JOHN P. MARQUAND
AND
MR. MOTO

Spy Adventures and Detective Films

RICHARD WIRES

BALL STATE UNIVERSITY

JOHN P. MARQUAND
AND
MR. MOTO

JOHN P. MARQUAND
AND
MR. MOTO

Spy Adventures and Detective Films

RICHARD WIRES

BALL STATE UNIVERSITY
Muncie, Indiana

Copyright © Richard Wires, 1990

Library of Congress Card Catalog No. 90-60342

ISBN 0-937994-17-0

90015 up

For Howell C., Bob E., and Alan W.
good friends and avid readers

Contents

Preface

In recent decades one of the most successful types of popular fiction has been the novel of espionage or international intrigue. Whether the works are complex in plot and somber in tone, like those of John Le Carré, or picaresque narratives of fantasy and violence, like those about James Bond, they have found a solid place in contemporary culture. Yet the spy story is a twentieth-century creation whose initial development and subsequent popularity have proven difficult for even the experts to explain. Most analysts now consider it to be a subgenre of the broad category usually called mystery fiction, which also includes detective stories, tales of suspense, and various kinds of thrillers, all existing both in separate or relatively pure form as well as in many hybrid or combination patterns. But all the other groupings can claim respectable practitioners long before the emergence of espionage literature.

Two phenomena help explain the late appearance of the spy story. Espionage is an old profession but one that until quite recently was never considered honorable: spies were people who deceived others, stole information, and worked only for personal gain—they were liars, thieves, and scoundrels. So how could they be made into fictional heroes? But with the growth of intense nationalism, military and naval competition, and worldwide imperialism in the late nineteenth century came new espionage and security services, highly publicized spy scandals, and sensational material for fiction writers. Stories of espionage and international intrigue acquired credibility and appeal because they followed the news reports. Changing conditions also permitted a different kind of hero: he might now be a counterintelligence agent, a dedicated patriot, or just a person who helps prevent hostilities. International tensions and the reactions they produced therefore led to the popularity of the espionage story.

Britons pioneered the new field in the early 1900s as international rivalries and war threatened Europe. A trio of classics stands out among the early works: Erskine Childers's *The Riddle of the Sands* (1903), Joseph Conrad's *The Secret Agent* (1907), and John Buchan's *The Thirty-Nine Steps* (1915). But nearly every writer of popular fiction at the time—including Arthur Conan Doyle, Agatha Christie, Somerset Maugham, John Dickson Carr, and others—at least dabbled in espionage tales. Two made it the basis of long and highly successful careers: William Le Queux and E. Phillips Oppenheim. Then came a major change. Eric Ambler's half-dozen fast-paced narratives revolutionized the spy story on the eve of World War II. Gone were the improbable heroes and overly contrived plots of earlier espionage fiction; gone also were all the easy assumptions of clear divisions between right and wrong. The contemporary spy story has its origins in those troubled years before and during the war.

John Marquand's contributions to the evolving genre have not been studied in detail because they came to be overshadowed by both his more innovative competitors and his own series of major novels in the late 1930s and 1940s. Yet the importance of his famous character in several popular media and the significance of his spy adventure stories in his life and literary career make knowledge of these six works valuable to many historians and readers.

Since the emphasis in this study is upon the novels themselves, and how their title character was altered to meet the requirements of the film industry, I have taken basic data about the author from standard biographies. But neither those works nor critical analyses of the writer's serious fiction have much to say about his light entertainments or magazine writing. In a few instances what they do include is inaccurate. With respect to the novels, I have used the original book titles rather than the serial titles, and I have cited what appear to be the most readily accessible reference editions. Other printings have been listed in the bibliography. I have also retained the older English spellings of Chinese proper names used in the novels. That pattern eliminates the need for double references and allows the analysis to conform to the original texts.

A number of colleagues and friends have offered valuable assistance and suggestions as the project went through development and revisions. Always constructive and encouraging, the comments and observations helped me resolve organizational problems and strengthen the presentation, although weaknesses still remain. For those I take complete responsibility, since it was impossible to incorporate all the advice I received without affecting too much the character and scope of this work. Among those I want especially to thank are the following: Gary Hoppenstand of the American Thought and Language department at Michigan State University encouraged the project from its beginnings; Robert Evans and Richard Brown of the English department at Ball State University commented upon various sections as they evolved; O. Alan Weltzien of the English department of Ferrum College, Virginia, critiqued the completed typescript with customary insight and thoroughness; Tetsumaro Hayashi of Ball State University explained the difficulty Marquand ran into concerning "Moto" as a Japanese name. I would like to express my appreciation also to the people of Ball State University Publication Services for their careful work. To all I have named and to many others who helped in countless ways to make this work stronger and more effective I wish to acknowledge my appreciation and gratitude for their interest and courtesy.

Richard Wires
Santa Fe, New Mexico

Introduction

John Phillips Marquand held an important place in American popular fiction from the early 1920s through the 1950s. After fifteen years as a highly successful writer of serials and short stories for magazines, Marquand won the Pulitzer Prize in 1938 for *The Late George Apley,* the first of more than a half dozen social satires on which his literary reputation rests. Yet he never completely abandoned the lighter forms of fiction at which he had become so adept. The causes of the dual levels in his subsequent career were both psychological and financial. He found that developing plots for adventure tales and historical romances provided a measure of mental relaxation, while the other requirements in writing such fiction presented no real difficulties, the genres themselves having little room for subtleties of characterization and motivation or richness of description. Marquand enjoyed creating such formula work at least enough to continue turning it out despite warnings that it diminished the stature he had acquired through his novels of manners depicting the society of New England. There was also a compulsiveness in his approach to writing that arose from a fear of financial insecurity that persisted long after he had become wealthy. He could not resist the large sums of money readily earned by sale of undemanding stories to the mass-circulation magazines. These are the circumstances under which Marquand wrote the six Mr. Moto adventures over a two-decade period. The works form so significant a part of his career, often paralleling the themes of his major novels, that their neglect by biographers and critics is unfortunate.[1]

Working with the Moto stories is neverless complicated by the existence of two different versions of Marquand's concept and character. Although Moto and his activities became familiar to millions through several media, the range itself attesting to the popular appeal of the character, he is probably best known from the prewar series of Hollywood films. Yet because the screenplays for the eight productions used little of the author's original material, they represent a substantially different approach to both characterization and content. Hence an important aim of this inquiry is to explain how the publications and films are related but divergent.

Each story appeared first as a magazine serial—four in the *Saturday Evening Post* in the mid- and late 1930s, one in *Collier's* in 1941, and the sixth in the *Saturday Evening Post* in the mid-1950s—and was then released as a trade book. The series ranks among the most successful magazine fiction ever published. But Moto was not planned as a continuing character when he made his debut in a 1935 story. Sequels came in response to huge reader interest. Even during the economically depressed years of the later 1930s, the official circulation of the *Saturday Evening Post* stood at more than three million, Americans finding the five-cent price a good entertainment investment. Recognizing the stories' effects on readership and advertising revenues, the magazine's editors continually pressed the author for further adventures, agreeing to pay exceptional sums for original publication rights. Although sales of the subsequent hardcover editions were profitable for his publisher, Little, Brown and Company of Boston, they never approached the high figures recorded for the author's serious fiction. Only with the paperback revolution during and after the war did sales of books reach extraordinary numbers; new paperbound editions kept the works in print for years and include a recent reissue of good quality.[2] Thus over the years many millions of magazine and book readers have followed the exploits of the likable agent.

Since a certain amount of confusion arises from variations in some of the titles, affecting the first and last two stories, it is helpful at the outset to note the principal titles one may encounter:

Serialization Title	Original Book Title	Paperback Title
No Hero	Same	*Your Turn, Mr. Moto*
Thank You, Mr. Moto	Same	Same
Think Fast, Mr. Moto	Same	Same
Mr. Moto Is So Sorry	Same	Same
Mercator Island	*Last Laugh, Mr. Moto*	*Last Laugh, Mr. Moto*
Rendezvous in Tokyo	*Stopover: Tokyo*	*Right You Are, Mr. Moto*

The publisher's aim was obviously to include the words "Mr. Moto" in order to unify the titles of recent reprintings. There are also occasional references in studies of Marquand to other names for some of the stories.[3] It might be noted as well that only two film titles, *Think Fast,*

Mr. Moto and *Thank You, Mr. Moto,* were carried over from the magazine and book publications. None of the other six prewar films used the author's titles or plots. For clarity and accuracy the works are normally identified in this study by the titles of the original book editions.

Other decisions in matters of style may also warrant explanation. The manuscripts were completed long before they appeared in the magazines, unlike many nineteenth-century serializations written piecemeal as deadlines loomed, and were intended for subsequent book as well as magazine publication. Therefore it seems reasonable and proper to refer to the works as books, rather than as serials, since the book editions are the more durable format and are readily available. The choice also conforms to the author's own preference. A second point involves the question of whether they should be called tales or novels. If the customary distinction must be imposed, the works are clearly tales or stories, with the possible exception of the last, for they lack the novel's substantive depth. But it seems unnecessary to adhere to any such scholarly distinction in this instance. The discussion makes evident the limited nature of most of the narratives, and occasional reference to them as novels should therefore not be misleading.

Proper description or classification of the works has been obscured by repetition of a common error. The plots do not fall into the branch of mystery fiction called the detective story; there is no concern with murders or other criminal acts occurring among ordinary citizens; the works do not feature a police investigator or private sleuth solving puzzling crimes. Moto was not a detective as that word is usually understood; he was an intelligence or counterespionage agent of imperial Japan. His assignments involved the protection of top government secrets, military plans, and other national interests against networks of enemy spies. Yet he has frequently been erroneously identified as a detective; the writings about him are therefore sometimes called detective stories. Probably the confusion arose from the belief that the screen characterization followed the author's original concept. Among those who have made or perpetuated the mistake, however, are writers who ought to know the printed material.[4]

The author himself referred to his stories as mysteries,[5] a suitably inclusive term, but perhaps a more apt label might be adventures, for action usually prevailed. Some come close to being thrillers.[6] As a group his narratives are filled with challenges, danger, surprises, duplicity, mistakes, romance, tricks, coincidence, disguises, and stakes of the greatest importance to the contenders. Although the mix

3

of such elements varies considerably from story to story, making the works dissimilar in tone and character, a common setting throughout the series is the world of international espionage. If we consider mysteries the best designation for the broad genre, as specialists in the field now do, these narratives belong to the subcategory set aside for spy stories. They appeared at a time when such works were still relatively new and unfixed in form; they clearly show evidence of being hybrids created from other subgenres through cautious experiments. Thus it is their interest as early examples of a now well-established and highly popular type of writing that makes them worthy of re-examination today. Fiction offering spy motifs treated with any degree of realism won readers only gradually in the years just before World War II as the public slowly adjusted to deepening world tensions and expected even its lighter fare to reflect actual conditions. Marquand was neither a major innovator in the emerging subgenre nor a conscious advocate of the new stark naturalism, both roles that Eric Ambler may justly claim,[7] but he deserves to be remembered and have a place among those who pioneered realistic spy fiction in the 1930s. The nature and extent of his contributions become evident when his writings are studied as a body of work.

Filmmakers in Hollywood quickly saw both the entertainment value and the potential awkwardness in producing motion picture versions of Moto's spy adventures. Studios at the time desperately needed good story material and especially welcomed action and romantic fiction that had already won widespread title or character recognition. In that respect the Moto tales seemed ideal for Hollywood to render as films. But how receptive would American audiences be in the politically troubled late 1930s to productions making a hero of a Japanese intelligence or government agent? The solution to the problem involved altering his image from that of a highly nationalistic counterspy to one of an internationally famous detective. Moto simply became a variant of Charlie Chan in the film adaptations of Hollywood. The films proved to be enormously popular and were seen by millions of people. Yet those who know only the motion pictures may assume incorrectly that the film depictions are relatively faithful dramatizations of the magazine serials and books. Even a number of respected film scholars have shown themselves to be unfamiliar with the characterization in and content of the printed works. Because the films represent a visual medium and a generally different body of material, thereby forming a contrast to the serials and books, they warrant a separate analysis and evaluation based upon cinema criteria and film techniques.

Discussion of the interrelated topics of this study has been divided into four parts. In the first section Marquand's career is briefly surveyed in order to place the Moto stories in that context. Then the original narratives are examined. The texts used are those of the book editions, which are the most accessible and therefore allow easy reference, and which do not differ from the magazine serials, except in minor ways or where titles were altered.[8] The third part deals with important questions of theme and characterization and also compares the stories with respect to their construction and quality. Consideration of the film productions constitutes the fourth section. The most significant points and observations from those discussions are then underscored in a short summary and conclusion.

NOTES

1. By far the most scholarly study of Marquand's life and work is Millicent Bell, *Marquand: An American Life* (Boston: Little, Brown and Co., 1979), since the author had access to all Marquand's papers and his publisher's files. Stephen Birmingham's *The Late John Marquand: A Biography* (Philadelphia: J. B. Lippincott Co., 1972) is an earlier popular biography that differs in some details from Bell's better-researched work. Birmingham nevertheless benefitted from interviews with people who knew Marquand. Also useful is the *New Yorker* profile by Philip Hamburger published as *J. P. Marquand, Esquire: A Portrait in the Form of a Novel* (Indianapolis: The Bobbs-Merrill Co., Inc., 1952). Two other solid books focus on analyses of his fiction. John J. Gross, *John P. Marquand* (New York: Twayne Publishers, Inc., 1963) concentrates on the author's major novels, however, and has little to say about the Moto stories. There is more on them in C. Hugh Holman, *John P. Marquand* (Minneapolis: University of Minnesota Press, 1965), but still not a sizable coverage.

2. Little, Brown and Co. reprinted all six books in paperback during 1985 and 1986. The first two works in the series appeared in 1985; the other four books were issued in 1986.

3. *No Hero* or *Your Turn, Mr. Moto* has sometimes been referred to as *Mr. Moto Takes a Hand*. Bell, p. 249, and Birmingham, p. 305, both erroneously give the latter as the work's title for its serialization in the *Saturday Evening Post* in 1935. *Stopover: Tokyo* was apparently issued in paperback at one point under the title *The Last of Mr. Moto*. See Holman, p. 47. That title may have been dropped because the publisher thought some other writer might at some time obtain permission to continue the series.

4. One example of the misidentification of the stories as detective or crime fiction illustrates the problem. Jacques Barzun and Wendell H. Taylor mention

the Moto books in their annotated bibliography entitled *A Catalogue of Crime* (New York: Harper & Row, Publishers, 1971) and then dismiss them because they are not pure detective or crime fiction. Their observation is certainly correct, but the works should never have been included in their listing of crime and detective stories. Birmingham also refers to the character in the books as a detective: see pp. 67, 78, and 85. John Lardner called Moto a "Japanese solver of crimes" in the *New Yorker*; see issue for 9 November 1946, p. 117. See also *Saturday Evening Post*, 24 November 1956. p. 23; *Time*, 7 March 1949, p. 109; *Newsweek*, 7 March 1949, p. 94. It becomes clear from these and other references that many writers and critics did not know the Moto books at first hand.

5. "Why Did Mr. Moto Disappear?" *Newsweek*, 21 January 1957, p. 106.

6. An informative analysis of thrillers is available: Ralph Harper, *The World of the Thriller* (Cleveland: The Press of Case Western Reserve University, 1969). Even the Moto stories that come closest to being thrillers lack a certain intensity and deliberate excitement that are hallmarks of the form. Chase sequences and rapid shifts in locale occur in several of the tales, but such elements were not typical of Marquand's story lines. The thriller form itself has also become more varied and subtle since its emergence as mass-appeal reading around the turn of the century.

7. Eric Ambler is widely recognized as creating the realistic spy novel in a half-dozen works published in the later 1930s in Britain: *The Dark Frontier* (1936), *Background to Danger* (1937; called *Uncommon Danger* in Britain), *Epitaph for a Spy* (1938), *Cause for Alarm* (1939), *A Coffin for Dimitrios* (1939; called *The Mask of Dimitrios* in Britain), and *Journey into Fear* (1940). His first book was conceived as a parody of the popular thriller form, but his approach soon became more serious and sophisticated as he developed the field's possibilities, and some of the later titles are now regarded by readers as classics.

8. There is evidence that Marquand made some changes at his publisher's request before the books appeared. But he generally resisted altering the texts the magazines used because he begrudged spending time on revisions of his light fiction. Page citations for the Moto novels refer to these printings: *No Hero* (Boston: Little, Brown and Co., 1935), *Thank You, Mr. Moto* (Indianapolis: The Curtis Publishing Co., 1977); *Think Fast, Mr. Moto*, in *Mr. Moto's Three Aces: A John P. Marquand Omnibus* (Boston: Little, Brown and Co., 1938); *Mr. Moto Is So Sorry* (Indianapolis: The Curtis Publishing Co., 1977); *Last Laugh, Mr. Moto* (Boston: Little, Brown and Co., 1986); *Stopover: Tokyo* (Boston: Little, Brown and Co., 1957).

I

Marquand and Moto

CREATION AND DEVELOPMENT of the Moto series formed part of a critical transition in Marquand's personal and professional life. Physically and mentally restless from the breakdown of his first marriage and continually anxious about the direction of his work, Marquand welcomed new scenes and challenges during the mid-1930s, traveling to unfamiliar regions of the world to absorb usable backgrounds and struggling toward completion of his first major novel. To place the Moto stories within that context therefore requires an understanding of several key aspects of Marquand's life and work. Financial constraints during his adolescence and then marital problems later so affected his outlook and approach to writing that knowing something of such circumstances is essential to explaining the origins and continuation of the adventure series. Another point of consideration involves his serious fiction, for the author's literary reputation rests on works quite different from his popular espionage stories, though at times he pursued both genres simultaneously, on occasion even using similar themes and conflicts in both his major and minor works. A final insight derives from seeing the relationship between the writer's love of travel to exotic lands and his use of such experiences as the inspiration for his adventure tales. Nearly all the locales and scenes of the Moto stories are traceable to the author's travel notes. From each of these three significant topics come valuable insights into the author's motives and methods.

The circumstances of Marquand's childhood and adolescence played a crucial part in forming his personality and help explain the presence of a recurring theme in so many of the Marquand stories and novels. Although he was born in Wilmington, Delaware, on 10 November 1893, his father having taken work as an engineer there, the

Marquands had lived in New England since the early 1700s.[1] When his father, by then a New York broker, lost his money in the 1907 panic, the boy's life was profoundly disrupted, for he was sent to relatives in Massachusetts, where Marquand learned that genteel poverty, in proper New England society, meant pain and disappointments.[2] He nevertheless managed to finish Harvard in 1915 and then worked for local newspapers. During the years between 1906 and 1918 he saw military service on the Mexican border and later was sent to France. After the war he wrote briefly for the New York *Herald Tribune* and then joined an advertising firm for a while. But when he decided to pursue a writing career, having completed and sold a short story with little effort or trouble, he quit the agency to work on a novel.[3]

The Unspeakable Gentleman is a romantic spy story serialized by the *Ladies' Home Journal* and then published in book form by Charles Scribner's Sons in 1922. It possesses many thematic and structural qualities that Marquand used in his Moto stories and in his more serious social satires. The tale is set in Massachusetts in the early 1800s as narrator Henry Shelton recalls events from his youth. His father was the "unspeakable gentleman" of the title and a "charming and deadly rascal" mixed up in intrigue—a highly complicated Bourbon political scheme that inevitably involves a beautiful French woman of mystery.[4] Both the plot and the characters now seem overly dramatic and implausible. Even the author later acknowledged that he disliked the work but felt it was the best he could achieve at the time. What is most noteworthy is its linkage to his later writings. From the very outset Marquand was obviously attracted to tales of espionage and conspiracy that he would learn to refine in Moto's international adventures. He also favored a structure in which a narrator looks backward and brings a present perspective to bear on past events. The device was subsequently used in both his popular stories and his social satires. Perhaps most revealing is his preference for characters of solid or even elite background who have been humbled or nearly brought to ruin by their fathers' or their own actions. Such Americans are found repeatedly in the Moto tales. In creating such protagonists Marquand retold his own history.

For fifteen years Marquand devoted all his energies to producing fiction for America's slick magazines. During that time he became a "front cover name" because his serials and short stories were so popular that people bought copies just to read Marquand's latest romance or adventure yarn. Marquand's output at times reached exceptional levels—twelve short stories published in 1929 and fourteen the next year—nearly all in the *Saturday Evening Post*.[5] His income kept pace with his fame. In the 1920s he earned from $500 to $3,000 for a story and between $30,000 and $40,000 for a serialized novel; in the depressed 1930s his income was $49,000 in 1934, a little less the next year, and more than $57,000 in 1936.[6] During 1936 he published more than in any other year of his career: two Moto novels, five stories, and some parts of *The Late George Apley* (then still in progress). Some of his expenses were high, particularly support payments after his first divorce, but he was certainly never in financial need, and his second wife was a multimillionaire. He himself earned an estimated $10 million from writing during his lifetime.[7] But his experiences growing up always made him worry about having enough money, even to the extent of complaining continually about costs and expenditures, so that those unfamiliar with his situation were undoubtedly misled about his finances. Perhaps it is that misconception that accounts in part for statements that he wrote the Moto stories just to support himself in the years when he was readying his serious novels. That was never true except to the extent that his own insecurity made him a compulsive worker.

There is little question that Marquand helped cause his marriages to fail. Self-centered and difficult to live with because of his demands, he also had a number of affairs, and then excused his wandering ways by blaming his wives' failings. Yet it seems clear that the qualities he admired in companions were not those he sought in a wife. Under the circumstances neither of the women Marquand married seems to have represented a wise choice. Each failed to provide the type of well-ordered and carefully managed domestic life that he found essential. Well-known among friends and associates as a man incapable of handling ordinary tasks, either at home or on travels, the writer relied on others to cope with both daily problems and special situations. And he expected those around him to be conscientious, punctual, and efficient in meeting his various needs and wishes. The same impatience with disagreement and detail that allowed him to be tugged one way and then another in his creative career let him accept his marriages' collapse when personal pressures and conflicts became too strong. Having been drawn initially to both women because of their family backgrounds and social positions, he came in time to regard each as a burden and threat to his freedom, and often in periods of despair he told friends that a writer should never marry.[8] Yet during the years when each marriage was faltering he fell in love with strongly independent women who led active and successful professional lives of their own. Both women saw quite clearly the weakness in Marquand that made him a poor marriage risk. It would appear in retrospect that the simultaneous commitment to slick stories and serious novels in his writing had a rough counterpart in his concurrent attraction to decorative socialites and career women.

Marquand married Christina Sedgwick in September 1922 just as his writing career got under way. Probably drawn to her in part because her family was socially prominent—her paternal uncle Ellery Sedgwick was editor of the *Atlantic Monthly* at the time—he quickly discovered she was hopelessly incapable of dealing with domestic routine. Totally impractical, languid, and given to nervous illnesses, Christina soon began to irritate Marquand, who objected to her habits, pretensions, and relatives.[9] Thus marital problems were among the reasons he seized the chance to travel to China in 1934 and then decided by late that year to tell friends he wanted a divorce. Christina obtained the decree in spring 1935. In the following years his obsession with money included unwarranted complaints about support payments for his former wife and their two children. Marquand's income for 1936 exceeded $57,000, but Christina received only $15,000.[10] Even though the percentage was not burdensome, the obligation itself was inescapable, so he worried about sufficient income. The situation undoubtedly helps explain Marquand's subsequent great productivity that included the creation and subsequent regular appearances of Moto.

But there had also been a more hidden reason for Marquand's dissatisfaction with his first marriage and pursuit of a divorce. In 1934 he was in love with a young family friend, Helen Howe, to whom he wrote often as he traveled in the Far East.[11] Nothing came of the affair. A perceptive person and herself a writer, Howe recognized the undesirable traits in Marquand, including a lack of simple social tact. She fell out with her erstwhile suitor when, without invitation or warning, he brought a young woman to see her. The visitor proved to be his prospective second wife. Howe later included a character in her novel *We Happy Few* that is a rather unkind portrait of Marquand.[12] His pattern of involvement with Howe during the time his first marriage was failing was repeated when his second marriage also began to falter and Marquand took a long-time mistress. That situation was even more closely associated with the Moto stories and the struggle to shape the writer's career.

When Marquand returned to China in mid-summer 1935 he again visited Peking and there met Adelaide Ferry Hooker, the heiress who eventually became his second wife. Marquand left for America while Hooker and her sister Helen continued to Europe on the Trans-Siberian Railway. Marquand had told the young women about his Mongolian adventure the previous year, prompting Adelaide to insist that they too should first make a brief journey to Mongolia. She was obviously fascinated by the writer whose romantic novel *Ming Yellow* had helped inspire her own travels.[13] They saw each other often in New York that fall and the following year. But neither was inclined to rush into marriage: their wedding did not take place until April 1937, after a twenty-month period of companionship.[14] A 1925 graduate of Vassar, Hooker had remained single and was well into her thirties when she married Marquand. Yet her reasons for marrying certainly seem less complicated and selfish than his. Several conditions suggest the author's egocentrism: he desperately needed someone to take charge of his personal life; Hooker and others noticed how much she physically resembled Marquand's first wife; he welcomed the security her wealth and social connections would provide.[15] Both partners nevertheless contributed to the gradual breakdown of the marriage. Convinced that she had creative talents for which she needed an outlet, Adelaide sometimes pursued activities that embarrassed or annoyed Marquand, especially when they involved her efforts to influence or shape his career.[16] Throughout their marriage she was extremely ambitious for her husband, pressing him to concentrate on work of high quality, and holding jointly with him a number of key copyrights.[17] Despite three children and outward appearances, the marriage slowly deteriorated. Marquand took a mistress late in 1941 and often neglected the unhappy Adelaide. Suspecting his infidelity but rejecting separation, she complained and caused difficulties, often drinking excessively, and becoming overweight. After some fifteen years, and still carrying on his longstanding affair, he sought a divorce, which she steadfastly refused to grant. Marquand finally obtained a Nevada decree in late 1958. Adelaide drowned accidentally in her bathtub while drunk in 1963.[18]

For years during his marriage, Carol Brandt was the writer's secret paramour. Marquand first met Brandt in Paris during summer 1926. Then twenty-three and married to would-be writer Drew Hill, she charmed him with her vitality and independence, qualities he found totally lacking in his wife, who had proclaimed herself an invalid during the couple's visit abroad. Both often felt at loose ends—Brandt spending some of her lonely hours writing a flapper novel called *Wild*—but each enjoyed the other's company. Marquand also learned an important writing method from Brandt. One day at a house party outside Paris she demonstrated how a good typist like herself could easily keep up with Marquand's dictation and save him hours of labor. Always comfortable telling stories and anecdotes, he enjoyed talking and liked the method for its speed, using it thereafter whenever possible. When they returned home they saw each other from time to time.

Marquand and Hill had the same literary agent, Carl Brandt, who also arranged publication of *Wild* for Carol. After Hill's death in a boating mishap in May 1929, Brandt got the young widow a trainee job with another literary agent in New York, and in May 1931 she married the somewhat older Brandt. At the time she disregarded warnings that he often drank too much. But Carol would never leave him, despite his alcoholism, and they remained married until his death in 1957. In the meantime she built a highly successful career of her own before the war. Changing fields to avoid any possible conflicts of interest after she married Brandt, she became Metro-Goldwyn-Mayer's East Coast story editor, Louis B. Mayer providing her with an annual salary of $50,000, plus expenses and a chauffeur-driven car for use around New York.

Carol's whole manner—her attractive personality and easy naturalness, her professional skills and businesslike efficiency—appealed to Marquand. He spent much of his time with the Brandts as he waited for his first divorce. Although Marquand continued to profess friendship for Brandt, relying heavily upon his advice and support during troubled periods, he and Carol became lovers late in 1941.[19] Many of their intimate friends were already convinced that Marquand had used Carol as the model for the character he called Marvin Myles in *H. M. Pulham, Esquire,* portraying her as a beautiful and energetic advertising executive. Brandt knew of the affair between his friend and his wife, but all conspired to keep knowledge of it from Adelaide. She seems never to have suspected the identity of her husband's mistress.[20]

Carol had a part in creating both the first and the last of the stories featuring Moto. Each work owed its development to the author's physical and emotional restlessness during the final stages of his marriages. In 1934 when he returned from China he stayed with the Brandts and dictated the initial Moto narrative to her. After Adelaide refused to grant him a divorce in the mid-1950s, Marquand accepted a commission to write one more adventure about Moto. After visiting Asia to update his background knowledge, Marquand joined Carol in

Europe, where she took dictation of Marquand's new story. Their daily work together on the manuscript of the final Moto novel marked a break for each from an awkward marriage. By then they had also been lovers for more than a dozen years. Brandt died in 1957, about a year before Marquand's divorce from Adelaide. After Marquand's divorce, Carol repeatedly refused his proposals. He always insisted that she not continue working, but Carol had become active in running the agency during Brandt's illness, an involvement she was unwilling to relinquish.[21] Certainly Carol recognized well the selfishness that had in part caused the breakdown of Marquand's marriages. He apparently also proposed to one or two other women after her refusals. But Marquand was still single when he died of a heart attack at sixty-six in July 1960. That same summer Carol married a successful attorney.[22]

Marquand remains best known for his gentle social satires that generally focus upon upper-class New England. In a series of novels beginning with *The Late George Apley* in 1937 and ending with *Women and Thomas Harrow* in 1958 he analyzed an old society in transition. The three earliest works hold special interest here because they appeared during the same years as five of the Moto tales. And Marquand's final narrative in the adventure series came toward the end of his life when he was planning his last major novel. Because the author pursued both levels of his writing career in such an interwoven pattern, some knowledge of the development and reception of his serious fiction is necessary for understanding the events concerned with creation of the popular espionage stories, although detailed discussion of his novels of manners lies beyond the scope of this study.

The Late George Apley earned its author the Pulitzer Prize in 1938. Although he began the manuscript in 1934, Marquand set aside for more than a year what he still called his "Boston novel," resuming work toward the end of 1935. In the interval he traveled abroad extensively, went through a divorce, and wrote stories he could market quickly. The latter included Moto's first two adventures. During all that time his friend and adviser, Alfred M. McIntyre of Little, Brown and Company, urged him to finish the promising novel. Marquand nevertheless did not complete the manuscript until autumn 1936. He had meanwhile become involved in the struggle that those around him waged for many years to control his image and shape his career. Marquand later felt his agent should have made him concentrate more on the project, and he never forgot that Bernice Baumgarten at Brandt and Brandt had slighted the final manuscript, but his annoyance probably served to mask his own uncertainties during the mid-1930s.[23] He and nearly everyone else worried about how the public would receive a subtle novel so different from his adventure tales and formula romances.[24] Yet the collective anxiety was unnecessary: the work was an enormous success. Excerpts from *The Late George Apley* appeared in the *Saturday Evening Post*. Just as that series ended in January 1937 the book was released. Despite the magazine version the book sales were outstanding—nearly 33,000 hardcover copies were sold during 1937, and sales eventually reached about 50,000 copies[25]—giving the author his first big success and bestseller. Those who had earlier voiced concerns about the work's marketability soon were proclaiming their foresight in having recognized just what the readers wanted.[26] Critical reception was also favorable, and the Pulitzer Prize seemed to cap the acknowledgment of Marquand's emergence as a serious novelist of manners.

Marquand followed up his triumph with two more books about changing New England: *Wickford Point* (1939) and *H. M. Pulham, Esquire* (1941). Realizing the importance of his second major effort, he labored hard to give *Wickford Point* both style and substance, but its sales proved to be somewhat disappointing. A shortened version appearing in the *Saturday Evening Post* undoubtedly cut into the book sales. Only about 40,000 copies were sold—fewer than its predecessor—and Marquand again worried about money.[27] Yet the novel is significant because it is more closely autobiographical than any of his other fiction. Narrator Jim Calder is a successful writer for magazines who has the same pride of craftsmanship and career anxieties as Marquand himself. But in 1941 Marquand had every reason to be pleased with *H. M. Pulham, Esquire*. The novel appeared in February, sold more than 50,000 copies in six months, sold another 157,000 in a Book-of-the-Month-Club edition, and was banned in Boston. It supposedly portrayed the city's women in an offensive way. The incident certainly had one unforeseen repercussion: Marquand somehow felt Harvard officials were partly responsible for the ban and left his manuscripts to Yale rather than Harvard.[28] The wartime and postwar novels that continued his analyses of social change were successful financially but vary somewhat in quality. *So Little Time* (1943) is not strong; weaker still is *Repent in Haste* (1945). But he then turned out a trio of solid works: *B. F.'s Daughter* (1946), *Point of No Return* (1949), and *Melville Goodwin, U.S.A.* (1951). *Thirty Years* is a collection of his fiction and other writings published in 1954. The last of the serious novels, *Sincerely, Willis Wayde* (1955) and *Women and Thomas Harrow* (1958), are also among his best works. In between them came *Stopover: Tokyo* in 1957, Moto's final appearance in print.

Several points with respect to Marquand's major fiction warrant brief note. During the decade from the appearance of *The Late George Apley* through publication of *B. F.'s Daughter* the total sales of Marquand's books reached about 2.6 million copies in all the various editions.[29] The author's obsession with personal finances diminished with such solid success. A second insight is that he was never good with titles, and most of his books had to be titled by his publisher.[30] But many of the novels became successful films, Marquand greatly enjoying his visits to Hollywood, even though he contributed little to the scripts.[31] Sales of motion picture rights to his novels and payments for related services nevertheless added greatly to his income. That he was not always pleased with the film treatments had much to do with the shift in media. A novelist of polite manners who dealt in class and regional subtleties, he focused many of his works on times of crisis or crucial junctures, when his characters through recollection come to realize how they got there. Neither the structure nor the action of such novels suited them for ready transformation into screenplays. By far the most important point concerning his major fiction is the debate over magazine serialization of the novels that raged for many years. The controversy pitting his agent against his publisher found the author himself vacillating and ineffective, complaining about the effect that shortened versions of his works had on his reputation and on the novels' character and book sales, but long unwilling to assert himself by making a decision and enforcing it regardless of pressure.[32] Arguments over serializations of his serious novels were therefore closely related to the whole struggle over whether he should continue to write magazine or popular fiction of any sort. That conflict involved the Moto stories throughout the series.

The importance of Marquand's travel experiences in the development of the Moto tales was enormous. His military service had given him an introduction to foreign travel, but with his success as a writer in the 1920s he began to make journeys as often as possible, always preferring the romantic and exotic over the more ordinary places. The deep emotional appeal that strange and distant lands held for the proper New Englander reflects the similar sorts of dichotomies found in his writing and love affairs. Certainly the creation of adventure stories allowed him to use his knowledge and impressions without having to acquire and demonstrate the type of expertise expected of the serious novelist using foreign settings. When Marquand came to realize in the early 1930s that he needed new locales to freshen his work, an unexpected opportunity to travel to China determined the exact course of change, for the insights gained from two trips in the mid-1930s led to his writing the Moto stories. Marquand became fascinated with China and especially loved Peking. He readily admitted in a 1949 interview that he felt comfortable working with northern China as background but not as substance.[33] For his major novels he dealt only with people and locales that had been familiar to him all his life.

Marquand created Moto to help fill a void left by the death of Earl Derr Biggers and the end of the stories featuring that author's Charlie Chan. The Chinese-American detective had become so enormously popular by the time of Biggers's death in April 1933 that editor George Horace Lorimer soon sought a replacement figure for readers of the *Saturday Evening Post*. He therefore offered Marquand both expense money and a cash advance to enable him to visit the Orient to gain background. Upon learning of the offer in February 1934, Marquand became enthusiastic about the opportunity, noting that "it means that I shall get a new slant on a lot of things, and they believe it will make me their fiction expert on China."

> They now want a new Chinese character and a Chinese background, particularly as they believe that the Orient will soon be on the front page in the news and will be for a long while. They have hit upon me as the boy to do it, and they want me to pack right off to China—preferably Peking. Aside from all other considerations this excited me a good deal, because it is primarily important business, a part of my profession and an offer which I don't think I'd refuse under any circumstances.[34]

Marquand understandably proved to be a close observer, tireless listener, good questioner, and careful recorder during his travels in Asia. The notebook he kept provided the material for many of his adventure stories, which brought him new readers and further wealth, while the insights he gained added greater sensitivity to his more serious writings.[35] For these reasons it is helpful to note his itineraries and reactions.

Even while aboard the *Empress of Japan* in early March 1934 the curious Marquand quizzed passengers and crew. At mid-month he was back briefly in Hawaii and again liked the islands' exotic mix. The Marquands had lived in Hawaii during the winter of 1931–32, the author recording the local color for future use as story backgrounds, but Marquand had left Hawaii hurriedly when his mother died in May 1932.[36] Japan provided his first new experience and yet held little attraction for Marquand. Perhaps if he had seen Tokyo before the devastating 1923 earthquake, had arrived late enough for spring to have taken hold, or had ventured beyond Tokyo into more traditional Japanese areas, he would have had a less negative impression of the nation. But he felt both fascinated and repelled by what he considered to be the capital's parody of Western civilization and by what he saw of its oppressive political atmosphere. Japan would seldom be portrayed sympathetically in his stories despite the creation of Moto. A chance view of the puppet premier of Manchukuo at the famous Imperial Hotel in Tokyo nevertheless struck Marquand as an incident worth using in a story. Still he did not linger in Japan any longer than was necessary. Soon he saw things in both Korea and Manchuria under Japanese control that reinforced his first ideas. He traveled by train from Seoul to Mukden, where he heard advice and tales from a *New York Times* reporter who had covered the area for years, and then made a sidetrip to Hsinkiang (Hsinking) in Manchukuo, where he noted how much the new Japanese overlords were doing to transform the valuable region.

Several insights and stories acquired from foreign newsmen in Mukden found their way into the fictional accounts he later produced. One prediction he heard repeatedly was that Japan and Russia would be at war within five years. Japanese encroachments into north China seriously worried the Russians. He also learned that the Japanese were obsessed with spying, and Marquand himself attracted their interest. Nearly everything in the sensitive border region had military significance in Japanese thinking, and every foreigner became an object of distrust or suspicion. Marquand did not miss the point that international intrigue involving real or imagined rival agents and clever counterintelligence operatives would be dramatic material for adventure stories set in northern China. He also learned details of how Chinese servants run a household from the wife of the American newsman who was his best informant. By working such arcana into his stories, Marquand achieved verisimilitude. The correspondent also introduced Marquand to an opium den and to Mukden's only nightclub for foreigners. From the same source Marquand heard stories of the White Russian refugee community in Harbin, "the Paris of Asia," and how well the Russians had lived in the 1920s before their assets were exhausted. In one of the Moto novels he had a Russian girl named Sonya repeat the description of Harbin as part of her life. Marquand clearly acquired a wealth of ideas and data during his rather brief stay at Mukden. He managed to use nearly all the information in one or another of his adventure tales.

Marquand left for Peking by train on 5 April. He took note that Japanese troops guarded each station, protected by barbed wire and sandbags, and officers sometimes came aboard to check Marquand's papers. By dark the train reached Shanhaikwan at the Great Wall, a town called "the first gateway of the realm" for its location, and Marquand recorded his impressions of the crowded Shanhaikwan station. Then he boarded the night train to Peking and was instantly captivated by the city. He wrote to a friend:

> I just got here this morning, but that is long enough to realize, even for a cynic like myself, that Peking is the most beautiful and delightful city in the world, though at last the world is passing it by.[37]

He spent eleven days exploring the city and visiting outlying points of interest, learning about political conditions from foreign correspondents and absorbing the atmosphere he was later to recreate in his stories. Yet he still longed for some type of real adventure. An opportunity presented itself when he met a Swiss news photographer who suggested a trip northward.

Walter Bosshard was a big and confident man who knew of a trader named Frank August Larson living in Inner Mongolia about four hundred miles north of the important merchant town of Kalgan. Marquand became certain he would now see a non-tourist Asia. They went by train to Kalgan, starting point for the old caravan route to Urga (Ulan Bator) and then still a major center of activity, as Marquand soon learned firsthand. Bosshard took him to see Adams Purpiss, a Russian merchant operating under a German charter, whose Kalgan headquarters fascinated Marquand. Entering a walled compound through a simple doorway, he found more than seven hundred camels in the courtyard, all being loaded with merchandise for the interior. Purpiss insisted his visitors continue their journey northward using his own driver and new Buick. Not only did the car attract attention along the route but it also served a purpose yet unknown to Marquand.

Larson had been in business about forty years and enjoyed a privileged position in Mongolia. By 1939 the Japanese had nevertheless forced him to leave, and later that year he visited Marquand in the United States. But in 1934 neither he nor his activities left the most indelible impression in Marquand's mind. The most memorable part of his stay in the remote area was a ten-day visit to the court of a local prince, Teh Wang of the West Senurt, whose territory lay in a region that both Japan and the Soviet Union regarded as vital to their military interests and were therefore seeking to control through pressure on its beleaguered ruler. The prince greatly admired the Buick and was given a ride. When Marquand and Bosshard returned to Kalgan, the writer asked why Purpiss had let them use the Buick. The merchant replied that he wanted the prince to see and desire the car, which would now be offered to him, but only in return for obtaining the right of caravans to cross his territory.[38]

Marquand had one further adventure before he ended a second long stay in Peking. Earlier he had met George Kates, a young sinologist from Boston studying in the city, and then he encountered Alan Priest, a curator at New York's Metropolitan Museum who was about to lead a small group to the Wutai Shan in Shansi province in search of Buddhist art treasures. Priest asked Marquand to join the party. Kates acted as interpreter for Priest. Others making the trip were rich Americans who had helped to finance it. Things did not go well, for the participants soon fell into two factions, reflecting their tastes and habits. Marquand became especially friendly with Ray Slater Murphy, a woman from New York in her thirties, the "R. S. M." to whom he dedicated *Thank You, Mr. Moto.*[39] Even after their return to Peking, the members of the group could not get along, and Kates recalled an awful farewell party.[40]

From Peking the author traveled to Shanghai and then boarded a ship for his homeward journey. He would later use his impressions of Shanghai in the story that introduced the Moto character. The sense of awe and inadequacy he had felt in China was summarized in a comparison he made upon his departure. Not only had he been a solitary stranger in a teeming new environment, but he also saw himself as a diver in the water, a figure in an element not his own who is accepted without interest. "But believe me you are not of that world."[41] He had met many Westerners who knew much about China and had listened closely to their advice and tales. Yet he understood instinctively at the outset that, whatever kinds of stories he might create to set against this colorful and complex background, he himself could never fathom or interpret it.

The impact of his trip to northern China nevertheless becomes readily apparent to readers of Marquand's adventure stories written in subsequent years. He was able to adapt experiences, incidents, and characters to work after work. Even though he never quite encountered the actual danger he seems to have sought—peril stemming from all the bandits and spies about whom he had been told—he knew how to build plots from the notes and impressions he had recorded. Upon his return home he set to work immediately on two manuscripts using the new background, one of which would feature his famous character (whose next three adventures also drew heavily upon the author's records and recollections of his journey). Clearly the money from the editors of the *Saturday Evening Post* proved to be very well invested.

Marquand's deep fascination with China led him to return in 1935 after traveling in Persia. Since the four-month trip began just as his divorce was granted, he was once more escaping from family turmoil, but the journey also took him away from his unfinished social novel. From the time of his departure in April until his return home at the beginning of September he had little chance for concentrated writing. He had made the trip to observe an archaeological expedition financed in part by some friends, perhaps intending to use the experience in his writing. There may have been a restriction against describing the expedition without approval of the sponsors, for he decided to leave and continue traveling eastward.[42] Marquand again felt drawn to China. Although he visited southern China for the first time, Marquand preferred the more turbulent north, so he returned to familiar Peking, where he met Adelaide Hooker during her stay there.[43] Revisiting the city also gave Marquand ideas and materials he used in Moto's second adventure, written that autumn.

Other Marquand travels played little part in the Moto stories. Hawaii is the principal setting for one of the works; the last of the prewar tales takes place around Jamaica.[44] The former story is interesting because Moto was operating in American territory, although no one at the time considered the implications of such spy activity. The Caribbean adventure, on the other hand, lacks the Oriental flavor and mystery of the previous stories. Japan is the main locale of the final work from the 1950s, but there is evidence that Marquand had considered placing at least some scenes elsewhere in Asia. By then familiar with more of the Orient from both wartime and postwar travels, trips made under government auspices or with magazine financing,[45] he tailored the account to where Moto might reasonably be working after the war.

In both their origins and contents the Moto stories form an integral part of Marquand's complex life and development as a writer. Two relationships are especially important. First, production of the adventure tales offered the author an escape from marital troubles, enabled him to continue earning high sums to assuage his unwarranted but real worries about money, and contributed to the extended struggle to shape his career and resulting reputation. Second, awareness of Marquand's incorporation of so much from his personal experience into all his writings, serious and popular, offers useful insights into the characterizations and plots he devised for the Moto spy adventures. Some connections are subtle, others more obvious. His young heroes often were recognizable versions of the author himself, reliving his youthful upheavals and consequent anxieties, trying to find or prove themselves despite all difficulties and reversals. Certainly such figures represent something more personal than what they appear to be—a professional writer's facile creation of typical romantic leads for slick magazine fiction. More easily traceable are the ties to the itineraries and incidents of the author's foreign travels that reveal much about how he conceived and constructed his popular tales. Specific instances in which these and other autobiographical sources influenced and shaped the Moto stories are illustrated and analyzed in the third part of this study.

NOTES

1. The Marquands were a Norman French family that left Guernsey to settle in New England in 1732.

2. Marquand rarely saw his parents during the following years. To find work as an engineer his father moved to California and then to Panama, and his mother followed loyally from one place to another. Eventually they returned to live once more in Delaware. His mother died in 1932, but his father lived to be nearly ninety. See Birmingham, pp. 103, 215. But his father's lifelong gambling caused Marquand a great deal of worry. He liked to see himself in both actual life and autobiographical fiction as the victim of his father's failures.

3. Marquand had submitted his first short story to the *Saturday Evening Post,* and it appeared in print in summer 1921. Birmingham, pp. 44, 301. The magazine thereafter became his principal outlet.

4. Holman, pp. 11–12.

5. Bell, p. 182.

6. Holman, pp. 13–14.

7. Ibid., p. 27. Marquand left a personal estate of about $1.1 million when he died in summer 1960. Bell, p. 477. By then he was divorced from his second wife.

8. Birmingham, p. 100.

9. Bell, pp. 200, 202; Birmingham, pp. 37, 39, 50–51.

10. Birmingham, pp. 14, 120. The biographer calls Marquand's divorce settlement with Christina "acrimonious and ungenerous." It scarcely caused Marquand any financial problems. See pp. 13–14.

11. Bell, pp. 183–85, 501.

12. Birmingham, p. 100.

13. The Hooker sisters had just completed with their mother a tour of Japan. Helen planned to be married in Europe to a man disliked by the Hookers. See Bell, pp. 245–46.

14. The engagement announcement appeared in the *New York Times* on 26 February 1937, p. 18. The wedding took place in mid-April 1937. Ibid., 18 April 1937, sec. 6-D, p. 1. See also Birmingham, p. 96; Bell, p. 262. For information on their marriage see Bell, pp. 237–38, 240, 245–46, 452; Birmingham, pp. 67–68, 91, 140–41, 144–45, 153.

15. Adelaide had an annual income when she married of only about $7,500. But her father headed Hooker Electrochemical Company, and the Ferry Seed Company provided her mother's fortune. Her father died in 1938. Thus Adelaide inherited from both parents and at her death had wealth totaling about $3 million. See Birmingham, pp. 4, 95–96, 298; Bell, pp. 239–40. The fact that one of her sisters was Mrs. John D. Rockefeller III suggests the social status her husband now had acquired.

16. Adelaide did have musical ability and had studied in Germany. She also liked interior decorating and at one point told friends she and her husband owned eight houses. But her widely publicized involvement during 1940–41 with the isolationist America First Committee using the name Mrs. John Marquand caused her husband many awkward occasions. See Bell, pp. 293–98; Birmingham, pp. 93–94, 117, 126–28.

17. The copyrights on some of Marquand's books beginning with *H. M. Pulham, Esquire* were shared with Adelaide as part of tax management. She received a quarter of the royalties. The author and his publisher approved the arrangement reluctantly because she was never a collaborator. But she undertook the copyediting of his manuscripts, and her careful work was valuable. Bell, p. 414; Birmingham, pp. 105–6, 140–41, 178.

18. Bell, pp. 417, 418, 434, 468; Birmingham, pp. 274–77, 298.

19. Birmingham, pp. 8–9, 53–59, 62–66, 128–30, 144, 276–80; Bell, pp. 165, 167–68, 416–17, 501.

20. Birmingham, pp. 136–39.

21. Brandt was sixty-eight when he died on 13 October 1957 from the long-term effects of alcohol abuse and emphysema. Carol had earlier joined the firm of Brandt and Brandt to keep it going for their son. Bell, p. 469; Birmingham, pp. 271, 273–74, 277–79.

22. Marquand suffered a heart attack in 1953 as well and knew his condi-

tion. Carol's third marriage occurred soon after Marquand's death but had been planned earlier. Bell, p. 432; Birmingham, pp. 245–46, 292–93, 296.

23. Marquand had shown in two earlier novels, *Warning Hill* (1930) and *Haven's End* (1933), the qualities that encouraged McIntyre. Thus there were precedents for his work in progress. But during the mid-1930s Marquand lacked self-confidence. Thus he was quite upset when his literary agency's initial reaction to the new manuscript seemed so negative. Bernice Baumgarten had risen from secretary to reader and then agent at Brandt and Brandt. She was the first person there to read the nearly finished manuscript and voiced her dislike of it. She may simply have been expecting Marquand's usual type of story or have failed to understand Boston's social strata and the work's subtleties. The Brandts thought somewhat better of the manuscript but still expressed misgivings to Marquand about its appeal and salability. Birmingham, p. 85.

24. Bell, pp. 249–50. McIntyre liked the manuscript but felt reader interest was limited and sales would be modest; others at the publishing house were even less optimistic; someone's suggestion that the author use a pseudonym especially angered Marquand. Editor George Lorimer also saw the work's value but ran along with the *Saturday Evening Post's* excerpts a warning that magazine readers should not expect the familiar Marquand romance. Birmingham, pp. 86–87. *The Late George Apley* ran in the *Saturday Evening Post* from late November 1936 until early in January 1937.

25. Bell, pp. 229, 255; Birmingham, pp. 81, 87–89; Hamburger, p. 6.

26. McIntyre exulted in the book's unexpected market and critical success and could not resist chiding the unfortunate Baumgarten. Bell, pp. 254–55.

27. *Wickford Point* was begun in summer 1937 and published in spring 1939. The author's disappointment in its sales led him to complain that he would always have to depend on magazine writing. That field must certainly have been tempting: in 1939 the *Woman's Home Companion* offered him $40,000 for a serial, and *Cosmopolitan* had proposed $5,000 for a story. Bell, pp. 271, 273–74, 275; Birmingham, pp. 111, 123.

28. Bell, pp. 276–77, 283, 284–85; Birmingham, pp. 141–43.

29. Bell, p. 394. *So Little Time* alone sold over a half-million copies in two months and represented a record for Little, Brown and Company. Ibid., p. 347. By the late 1940s Marquand was so famous that he was featured on the covers of both *Newsweek* and *Time* for 7 March 1949. The occasion was the publication of *Point of No Return*.

30. Birmingham, pp. 141, 165–66. Marquand's own troubles with titles did not prevent him from giving advice about them to the young Birmingham. Ibid., p. ix.

31. Marquand had early success with Hollywood. His story "The Right That Failed" was made into a 1922 film of the same name by Metro Pictures; Arrow Films made the story "Only Two of Us Left" into the 1923 film *High Speed Lee*. See Johnny Minus and William Storm Hale, *Film Superlist: 20,000 Motion Pictures in the Public Domain* (Hollywood: Seven Arts Press, Inc., 1973). His longest visit to Hollywood occurred when *H. M. Pulham, Esquire*

was being filmed. Bell, pp. 286–90; Birmingham, pp. 146–51. Adelaide's rejection of films as an inferior art may have helped convince the author that his novels had been poorly used by Hollywood. Birmingham, p. 194.

32. Three examples of what occurred may be cited. In the first, Marquand opposed serialization but gave in to Brandt's arguments and allowed it. *Wickford Point* ran 70,000 words in the *Saturday Evening Post* serialization, but the book from Little, Brown and Company had 190,000. Marquand left the cutting to Brandt. *H. M. Pulham, Esquire* was serialized in a skeletal version as *Gone Tomorrow* in *McCall's*. Marquand quarreled over that episode with Brandt. The author himself reduced *So Little Time* from 1,040 to 675 pages (260,000 words), which Brandt thought he could edit for serialization to just 80,000 words, but Marquand sided with McIntyre at Little, Brown and Company and opposed Brandt's idea. Such drastic cutting greatly altered the character of the original manuscripts. Bell, pp. 273–74, 276–77, 341–42.

33. Marquand told Harvey Breit in the interview, "I think I have the atmosphere of North China down pretty well," so that he could use it as background in *Ming Yellow* and the Moto stories, but he said he lacked enough knowledge to write about it. "An Interview with J. P. Marquand," *The New York Times Book Review*, 24 April 1949, p 35.

34. Letter from Marquand to Helen Howe, 11 February 1934, quoted in Bell, pp. 204–5.

35. The summary of his 1934 trip is adapted largely from material in chapter 12, "Journey to the East," in Bell's biography, pp. 204–21. Marquand's notebook of travel experiences is in Boston University's Marquand Collection.

36. Ibid., pp. 188–96. Marquand did almost no writing in 1932 and published only one story during 1933. Ibid., p. 198. Both his mother's death and his marital problems contributed to his malaise and to the eagerness with which he accepted the travel offer early the following year. Yet his income for 1933 was still $19,000 from his publications. Birmingham, p. 68.

37. Quoted from an undated letter to Helen Howe.

38. In 1939 Marquand recounted this trip in a paper called "Where Are You, Prince?" delivered before the Tuesday Night Club in Newburyport, Massachusetts. The author's fondness for the adventure led him to include the paper in his collection of writings entitled *Thirty Years* (Boston: Little, Brown and Co., 1954), pp. 395–408. Clifton Fadiman wrote an introduction for *Thirty Years*. Much later Marquand saw Bosshard once again. In April 1947 Marquand made a two-week "V.I.P." air tour that included China and Tokyo. During a one-day stopover in Peking he met Bosshard and several other old acquaintances. Bell, pp. 334–35.

39. The dedication read, "To R. S. M., that indefatigable traveller and sinologist."

40. Kates was able to recall much about Marquand in China when he was later interviewed by Bell. But the biographer noted that he did not seem to realize just how much the writer had been absorbing during their time together. Kates had also served as the novelist's guide to the antiquities of Peking. Bell, p. 501.

41. Ibid., p. 218.

42. Marquand was traveling with Mrs. Murphy. She had donated two cars to the expedition that he helped deliver. On 17 June 1935 they left Persia, flew by way of India, Siam, and Cambodia to Singapore, and proceeded by ship to Hong Kong. Mrs. Murphy went on with him to Peking. Ibid., pp. 229–37.

43. Ibid., pp. 236–38.

44. The Marquands visited Jamaica during a West Indies vacation in 1938. Nothing in the novel *Last Laugh, Mr. Moto* required any detailed knowledge. See discussion in chapter 2.

45. During the war Marquand worked part-time for the War Research Service compiling data on Axis use of biological warfare. In summer 1943 he traveled overseas for the War Department to describe war conditions; bad weather over the Himalayas prevented him from visiting Chungking as he had initially proposed. Bell, pp. 315, 318–19, 324, 327. In early 1945 Marquand toured Pacific fighting areas for the Navy Office of Public Relations, and in April 1947 he again toured the Far East for the United States government. Ibid., pp. 327–30, 334–35. The *Saturday Evening Post* paid the expenses of his summer 1955 trip when he spent nearly three weeks in Tokyo to acquire background for *Stopover: Tokyo*. See chapter 2.

II

The Moto Narratives:
Agents in Action

MARQUAND'S APPROACH to the construction of plots, choice of themes and character types, and handling of background color reveal much about his methods as a writer, the conventions of magazine serial fiction, and the reasons for the Moto tales' popularity. Acquaintance with the lighter works shows too that his commercial writing differed from his major fiction less in craftsmanship and style than in subtlety and depth. Knowledge of the original narratives also allows comparison of the concept and substance found in the printed stories with those devised for film treatments.

A work called *Ming Yellow* was the initial product of Marquand's Far East travels. Its development during summer 1934 barely preceded that of another story, *No Hero,* in which Moto first appeared. Since the publishing history of the two works is intertwined, and both reveal the author's attempts to deal with a new background, certain points concerning the earlier story require comment. Marquand seems to have completed the manuscript within about a month of his return home in 1934. While his agent was showing it to the waiting magazine and book editors, Marquand quickly finished *No Hero,* which was also circulated and then sold to the *Saturday Evening Post* during the autumn. In the two works the locale, character types, and plot are somewhat similar. The principal differences between them are more rapid pacing of the second narrative and its introduction of the figure who was to become recurring and famous.

Ming Yellow appeared in the *Saturday Evening Post* in six parts from December 1934 to mid-January 1935. In announcing its forthcoming publication the magazine stressed the exotic: "romance and adventure against the hard brilliance of bandit-infested North China, with rare porcelains and a lovely girl at journey's perilous end." The front cover of the issue in which it began carried the name of the author and story.[1] Although the work offers colorful background, the plot is quite weak, and the story often lacks excitement. The hero is an American newspaperman who prefers to mind his own business but almost inevitably becomes drawn into helping a fellow American caught up in trouble. Marquand's story line follows the quest for a piece of valuable yellow porcelain through the world of warlords and outlaws he had heard described but had not seen for himself in northern China. The notable strength of the work, one found in all his narratives set in the region, is its strong sense of atmosphere, recreated by the author from the notes and impressions of his travels. *Ming Yellow* achieved only moderate success for Marquand. Although the serialization was profitable, and *No Hero* was purchased by the magazine even before *Ming Yellow's* run, the book sales were disappointing. McIntyre had ready expressed to Brandt his mixed reactions to *Ming Yellow:*

> We doubt if the novel will add particularly to John's reputation but it is an excellent story of its kind, and I personally found it good reading; in fact, I read it from beginning to end without laying it down. John has an excellent style which lifts it a bit out of the class of ordinary adventure stories. We shall be glad to take it on moderate terms.[2]

Concerned upon learning of such views, Marquand wrote on 8 October 1934 to Roger Scaife, vice president of the publishing firm. Noting with respect to *Ming Yellow* that he was "under no great illusions regarding its artistic merit," he said he hoped to give Little, Brown and Company "something better" before too much time passed,[3] probably a reference to the neglected manuscript of what he liked to call his major "Boston novel." Fewer than two thousand copies of *Ming Yellow* were sold during its first month out.[4] Nor did it gain many readers after that.

For the other story using the new background, Marquand decided to shift the focus from mere lawlessness to the intense competition for control of northern China being waged by the country's more powerful neighbors. The situation offered unusual opportunities for a tale of intrigue and treachery, fiction that would seem believable to newspaper readers of the time, but one also posing difficulties in terms of establishing a suitable point of view. In 1931 Japan had taken advantage of China's internal weaknesses to occupy the mineral-rich province of

Manchuria and then create the puppet state of Manchukuo. The next step in Japan's military and economic expansion into northern China was to obtain control of adjacent areas, parts of Jehol and Inner Mongolia in particular, in order to block the Soviet Union from interfering in the region through Outer Mongolia or elsewhere. Thus the bitter rivalry between Japan and the Soviet Union could be an exciting background. But how might a popular American writer handle such a situation? He could sympathize with neither imperialist Japan nor the communist Soviet Union in their politics and aggressive ambitions. The author's eventual solution required a balanced approach: identifying with the Chinese in their plight, making certain his American heroes were patriots, devising plots in which the leading characters' common goal is always to prevent hostilities, implying that the Russians are most dangerous, and portraying his Japanese agent as reasonable. One must remember that Marquand had not planned a series, but the formula and guidelines served him well through half a dozen stories, letting readers accept the mysterious Moto as a character they might respect.

No Hero took shape rapidly with clerical help from Carol Brandt during Marquand's visit to the Brandts' summer home in 1934. On weekdays when she had her own work to do, she took his dictation in late afternoon and left him the typescript, which he then edited or revised the next morning; on weekends they worked together on the project throughout the day. By summer's end the story was finished.[5] Lorimer liked what Marquand had fashioned, and No Hero was purchased by the Saturday Evening Post for use in spring 1935. In its advance announcement of the serial the magazine carried a capsule description that included as many enticements to readers as possible:

> Casey Lee, war aviator and ocean flier, finds himself in Tokyo practically "on the beach." As a man without a country he interests the Japanese secret service, which is intent on discovering the whereabouts of a mysterious document threatening to upset the balance of sea power in the Pacific. More exciting, more romantic, more absorbing than the recently published Ming Yellow is this five-part drama of a man who cannot disown his heritage.[6]

The story ran in six parts, 30 March through 4 May 1935, instead of the five announced.[7] But it is impossible to say whether the run was extended because the adventure tale's popularity was boosting sales or because layout considerations made a change necessary. The cover of the issue with the first installment carried the words "Beginning NO

HERO by J. P. Marquand" in large letters; the story held the lead position, and the highly skilled F. R. Gruger began his long service in providing drawings to illustrate key passages in the prewar narratives.[8]

McIntyre barely concealed his disappointment over Marquand's continued neglect of the promised "Boston novel" but nevertheless agreed to publish *No Hero*. In a letter to Bernice Baumgarten at Brandt's agency dated 18 December 1934, McIntyre said he agreed with Brandt that *No Hero* was a story in the E. Phillips Oppenheim mold, well done for that type of adventure, "and it may be that in this field John's sales can be developed."[9] Yet McIntyre still held out hope that Marquand would finish the "Boston novel" by spring of 1935 for publication that autumn, with release of *No Hero* delayed a year. Instead, *No Hero* appeared as a trade book in 1935, and sales were not so encouraging as those of *Ming Yellow*.[10] Brandt meanwhile persuaded Twentieth Century–Fox to acquire the screen rights to *No Hero* during autumn 1935,[11] but the studio was apparently uncertain how to handle the property and never made the first story into a motion picture.

Marquand opened the novel with its narrator, Kenneth C. Lee, known as K. C. or Casey to friends, recalling events of the past year for a report that an acquaintance, James Driscoll, a Naval Intelligence officer, will forward with his own to Washington. By framing the main story in this way the author was able to portray the principal character as he emerged from the adventure a reformed man, to use Lee's comments to prepare the reader to like the mysterious Japanese agent, and to build interest by revealing that his report tells a story of espionage involving a beautiful girl and a secret of great importance to many nations. Lee's story began in Tokyo. A naval air hero and stunt flier now bitter and alcoholic from lack of work, Lee was to have made a solo publicity flight back from Japan, but instead found himself stranded and broke when the sponsor decided to cancel the project. One afternoon while drunk at the Imperial Hotel bar and eager to regain some attention, he loudly blamed his nation for his misfortunes and dramatically tore his passport in half, causing countrymen like Driscoll to leave the bar in disgust at his behavior. But a Japanese man wearing formal attire who had also heard the flier's remarks helped him to his room and introduced himself as Mr. Moto. A little later when Lee awakened he was informed that Sonya Karaloff was waiting for him and wondered if Lee had forgotten having invited her. As he returned to the lobby still rather drunk, he bumped into a Japanese officer watching a delegation from Manchukuo return from seeing the emperor, causing the angry officer to threaten an incident. Trouble was avoided when the beautiful Russian woman produced a signet ring Lee had seen Moto wearing earlier. Who was this White Russian with such power? Lee knew that "Japan was full of spies" and quickly assumed Sonya worked for Moto. Soon he learned he was right. Sonya took him to a restaurant where he received a proposal from Moto: he would get a special Japanese plane for his publicity flight to America in return for a favor. Moto explained that his government had information about a new type of battleship and wanted Lee to ascertain from naval personnel if the same data were known to the Americans. Lee accepted the offer and agreed to go to Shanghai.

It is interesting to note just how Marquand handled the problem of Lee becoming a Japanese spy without having to use that exact description. In his report Lee wrote that "I had never felt so completely friendless or so cut off from everything I had known," for he realized the job was not wholly creditable even though it seemed harmless enough. He went ahead with it because he had committed himself in good faith, not fully understanding all the implications, but admitting it was the kind of unpatriotic deal his countrymen would condemn. Such an explanation is plausible, though hardly convincing given the character's background and lack of naïveté, but it overcame an awkward narrative problem. Marquand had somehow to explain and yet gloss over activities that many readers would view as almost constituting treason on Lee's part. Certainly the author was more realistic when he allowed the woman to observe correctly that the hero had now joined her as a person without a country.

The next part of the story finds all three principal characters aboard a southbound steamship, Lee having received his carefully repaired passport and a ticket from Moto, who avoids his new agent so that no suspicion of his role or mission will arise. But during the night a frightened Chinese man named Ma quietly entered Lee's cabin; Ma said he would soon entrust Lee with a note and asked him to get it safely to James Driscoll or Wu Lai-fu in Shanghai. In retrospect the narrator sees that night as the turning point in his life: Ma's respect for Americans had shamed Lee. He even refused a drink. Readers may find the change in character to reveal national pride, self-reliance, and independence too abrupt to be anything but a space necessity. Yet it works well enough in this type of story. The change allows the hero to dissociate himself from the job he had accepted and become a free actor in the new drama that now rapidly unfolded. Moto admitted he was looking for some unknown person carrying information; when Ma was found murdered, Sonya said he had worked for her father and urged Lee to return to America quickly; Moto's men could find no message, which perhaps had been memorized, so he threatened to torture Lee; Sonya revealed the Japanese wanted her father's scientific papers and told Lee to swim ashore at Shanghai; with her help he jumped overboard and managed to reach Wu. All he took were his documents in an oilskin pouch and his valued whiskey flask.

Shifts in loyalties occurred rapidly in Shanghai as everyone scrambled for the message. Wu provided his guest with dry clothes but seemed to disbelieve Lee. Then for some reason he accepted the American's denial of knowing about a secret message. Lee next sought out Driscoll. But the intelligence officer reacted to him much as Wu had done, considering him a Japanese spy and drunkard, although Driscoll was also eager to get his hands on the message. Driscoll knew Ma worked for Karaloff and became intrigued when Lee told him Sonya was a Karaloff. After confiding that the missing information "may concern the entire balance of power in the Pacific," he offered expense money if Lee would play up to Sonya to learn what she knew. Driscoll continued to regard her as an agent working for Moto. Lee said he was no gigolo and would find things out in his own way. He thought Wu's sudden switch, at first working with Driscoll but then proceeding independently so he could sell what he learned to Japan or the highest bidder, showed that Wu knew something. Sonya then betrayed Moto to save Lee. Explanations of these developments later become clear to the narrator: Karaloff had invented a process for doubling the power of crude oil and thereby increasing twofold a ship's cruising range; Japan had agreed to buy the formula in exchange for arms sought by the anti-communist refugees living in Harbin; Tokyo had changed its mind after it thought it had all of Karaloff's data, but key information had been withheld, and through Wu Karaloff had next begun secret negotiations with the Americans; the crucial papers were now hidden but Sonya had just learned her father had been killed by the Japanese; Ma had suspected the hero would never part with his flask and had hidden the message in its detachable bottom. But things in Shanghai had gone badly. Wu's men had finally discovered the note and substituted another, which Lee had found but which Sonya claimed was not in Ma's characters, nor correct in naming his brother's village in northern China. Someone was already en route to the real hiding place. Lee mentions in his report that he tried a bit of deception himself by selling the false note to a seemingly gullible and grateful Moto.

The final events took place in the village some six hundred miles north. Lee had managed to borrow a two-seated plane from an old acquaintance now training pilots for China, knowing that it lacked the fuel capacity to return from their destination in territory occupied by Japan. At the brother's farm Lee and Sonya quarreled and the paper was torn. Lee burned his part and then, after they heard another plane landing, was allowed to destroy Sonya's. Moto then appeared oddly attired in a tweed golf suit and said he had bought knowledge of their whereabouts from Wu. He believed their statements about having burned the information, saying the loss helped Japan and America stay on good terms, and then got army fuel for their return flight. Sonya was with Lee when he saw Driscoll back in Shanghai. They agreed that Moto was certainly a government agent, but also a gentleman and man of honor, someone whom Americans could respect and perhaps even like.

A number of component qualities in *No Hero* suggest the patterns its genre demanded. The plot is carefully constructed and developed, though rather slow moving in approaching its climax, and attests to the author's sound craftsmanship, a skill he demonstrated throughout the series. When his dialogue occasionally takes an unexpected turn, as when the hero finds Ma dead and a shocked Sonya standing nearby, knife in hand, the exchanges seem to reflect a dated style. Here the introduction of some of the wisecracking banter of the period, with the initially surprised hero saying, "I am sorry. I'm afraid perhaps I have intruded," and continuing in that light vein, now rings false given the tense situation and purported attempt at realism. Most characterizations, solid without being too detailed, favor stereotypes. Thus the author created a romantic hero with an uncommon occupation and abilities, whose descent into self-pity is reversed through physical action and love. He also expresses the ordinary man's sense of surprise at finding himself involved in great events. As Lee observes in his account of what happened, "It only seemed to me incredible that a comparatively harmless person like myself, who, a few days ago, had not but self to think of, should be caught up in the edges of a completely fantastic snarl."[12] Not until the final story of the series would the hero ever be an American agent. The heroine is the prototype of those to follow—intelligent, beautiful, resourceful, and independent. Her role was an essential ingredient of all magazine romances. But Moto emerged as an unusual and intriguing man of mystery whose good will softened the awareness of his profession and whose activities could be further elaborated if Marquand wished.

32

Also important are two points that contributed greatly to the verisimilitude of the initial story. One is the author's realistic treatment of the world of spies and espionage, best examined from the perspective of the whole series, and the other is the manner in which he used his own experiences, most clearly seen as each of the stories is discussed.

Marquand's quite different feelings about the two nations he used as locales are readily apparent in *No Hero*. His genuine dismay at Japan's superficial westernization to the detriment of its own traditions had been increased by his annoyance with the constant Japanese suspicion of all foreigners. In the story he seemed to make the Imperial Hotel designed by Frank Lloyd Wright a symbol of the cultural mix that impressed him unfavorably. It figured again in the last of the Moto stories twenty years later, Marquand's reaction to it having scarcely changed.[13] He also patterned the Moto character after a type of semi-westernized Japanese person he had often encountered. Such people represented the human counterpart of the hotel's stylistic mixture. That is precisely why he made Moto seem quite ludicrous in Western clothes. Marquand felt much different about China. What gave his writing its sense of authentic atmosphere was his ability to weave his travel notes into his fiction and instill something of his enthusiasm and delight. Marquand knew the Imperial Hotel and had observed the arrival of a delegation from Manchukuo in 1934; Sonya's description of the White Russian exile community comes from what newsmen had told Marquand about conditions in Harbin; Marquand visited a Chinese village and had returned to the United States from Shanghai. Perhaps the scenes in Shanghai illustrate best how he conveyed to readers his fascination with China's rich mosaic and culture. Rather than describe things in detail, clearly impossible in the adventure format, he opted for sweeping romantic images, as when his narrator assures the reader, "I doubt if any city in the world is more amazing than Shanghai," and "Anything can happen in Shanghai."[14] The first four stories in the series rely so heavily on his travel experiences and recollections that they have a special sense of place greatly missed in the fifth prewar tale.

At the beginning of September 1935, Marquand returned from his second trip to the Orient, promising McIntyre to begin working hard. But his "Boston novel," to be titled *The Late George Apley* in final form, would vie for time with Moto; the editors of the *Saturday Evening Post* wanted a sequel. Although Marquand seemed optimistic about handling both tasks, he found the adventure story easier to write, completing the manuscript for his agent by December.[15] *Thank You, Mr. Moto* ran as six installments in the magazine during February and March 1936. Thus its serialization began just nine months after the last part of the original story had appeared. Newspaper advertisements placed by the magazine increased sales by a quarter of a million copies.[16] Adelaide told her family the magazine paid the author $30,000. When the second story proved to be as popular as expected, the publication offered $40,000 for another manuscript, which the writer began quickly and hoped to finish by summer.[17] The financially obsessive Marquand found it difficult to turn down such sums, of course, but time devoted to Moto stories slowed progress on other work. McIntyre without much enthusiasm agreed to a book edition of the second Moto.

For the setting of his second story Marquand again drew upon places he had visited. But the focus this time was much narrower, all the action taking place in Peking as confusion and rumor sweep the unprotected city and a Japanese army stands poised to enter it, using the turmoil as the pretext for intervention. Marquand was certainly familiar with Peking and the machinations of Japan. By concentrating his narrative in one locale, he produced a story lacking the mobility of his earlier tale, but highly effective in other ways. The pervasive atmosphere of tension and desperation, with both the local populace and various foreigners scrambling to safeguard their interests or improve their positions, adds immeasurably to the sense of excitement. And for the second appearance of Moto the espionage theme was more subtle.

An American expatriate named Tom Nelson is narrator of *Thank You, Mr. Moto*. Having arrived in China several years before the novel begins in the wake of some problem involving his law practice, he has immersed himself in Chinese culture. But in other respects he has drifted aimlessly, remaining uncertain about returning to his old firm, which knows he was blameless in whatever happened. At a party in the old diplomatic quarter, Nelson runs into Moto, whom he has met on a previous occasion. Moto suspects the quiet young man may be an intelligence agent and wonders if a book he is supposedly writing really involves Japan. Others at the gathering include Eleanor Joyce, authorized by an American museum to spend $200,000 for a set of eight Sung dynasty paintings, and Major Jameson Best, a former British intelligence officer who asks Nelson to dine with him that evening, although the American scarcely knows the man. Best turns out to be an adventurer deeply enmeshed in the dangerous factional strife of northern China. He has been working with a powerful warlord, Wu Lo Feng, helping his men infiltrate the city to pillage and create incidents, and with an agent of the Japanese extremists and expansionists, Takahara, who needs such violence as a pretext for a military occupation. But Best has somehow double-crossed the warlord and Takahara. As Nelson leaves the major's house that night he is annoyed to see Eleanor Joyce arrive and suspects her of having an affair with the disreputable Best. Deciding to return a few minutes later, he discovers the major shot to death and the woman still there but distraught. Moto then also appears, telling Nelson he is a Japanese agent, but opposed to Takahara. The killing is temporarily covered up. Nelson has become attracted to the woman, who may be a murderess, and wants to help a fellow American. But both are now in danger because Wu suspects Best may have told them of the scheme.

The plot skillfully interweaves the pursuit of the paintings with the unfolding of the political intrigue. A curio dealer named Pu has told Joyce of a Chinese painting for sale. But when Nelson takes her to see Prince Tung, a member of the old imperial family in whose house he thinks she will be safe, Prince Tung says the dealer is acting for Wu, who has gotten the set of paintings by looting a monastery and stealing from the prince. Until then the girl has not suspected she is negotiating for stolen art works. But at that point Wu's men invade the prince's house and take all three as prisoners to one of Peking's many deserted temples. There the final action occurs, Moto having been caught by Wu, so that everyone is present. Yet the prisoners manage to overpower their guards, Eleanor even disarming Wu, who has never credited a woman with courage and speed. When the freed group leaves the temple, Moto remains behind with Wu and his countryman Takahara, and later he admits he killed them. His explanation is simply that it was necessary. The incident not only shows that Moto can be ruthless in pursuing his objective—prevention of trouble in the city and action by the radical militarists—but also allows Nelson to remain free of any responsibility for the deaths. Moto alerts the local police to deal with Wu's men before they can cause violence in Peking. Other matters are resolved when Prince Tung agrees to sell his paintings to the museum and Nelson decides to return to his old law firm in America after the girl marries him. The novel ends as the young couple thank the polite little agent for all he has done.

Thank You, Mr. Moto has characteristics that clearly distinguish it from other works in the series written before the Second World War.

Without the physical action and rapid shifting of locale so typical of the thriller, the story relies more upon an element associated with the traditional mystery, a foreboding sense of danger among people who find themselves cut off from the world. The plot is also less complex and more plausible than others the author created for the series. It clearly derives from Marquand's long stay in Peking on his first journey: George Kates perhaps suggested the character of a young American exile immersing himself in Chinese culture; Alan Priest's quest for art treasures on behalf of a museum undoubtedly explains the mission of Eleanor Joyce; certainly Marquand recalled the group in Peking in dedicating the novel to his friend Mrs. Murphy. But the author also used the headlines of the period to good effect, for American readers knew generally what was happening in threatened Chinese cities, their minds easily supplying the background and images his words would only sketch. With its compactness and controlled tone, the story seems more serious in nature than the lighter and more action-oriented entries in the series. Such a perception earns the story a certain margin of respect over its fellow adventures. Further evidence of the work's strengths comes from the film version that appeared late the following year: the script tended in both its narrative lines and colorful characters to follow the book. Perhaps as a result the screen treatment stands as arguably the best production among the eight prewar films. Yet the adventure tale that soon followed *Thank You, Mr. Moto* had little of its believability and tautness.

Marquand's most productive year for publications was 1936. Part of that activity was a third Moto story completed in a short time, serialized immediately, and destined to become Hollywood's first film in the long and successful sequence. *Think Fast, Mr. Moto* ran in half a dozen parts in the *Saturday Evening Post* starting on 12 September 1936, just six months after the ending of *Thank You, Mr. Moto*. The magazine advertised it as "another adventure of sly, efficient Mr. Moto, the Japanese G man," giving it prominent cover space and the lead position for the initial installment.[18]

No particular problem arose concerning book publication of the third serial, which McIntyre thought better for his needs than the earlier Moto tales, but the publisher did not feel justified in improving contract terms. On 13 July 1936 he wrote to remind the author's agent that "we still have a long way to go before we can say that we have put over the Mr. Moto stories."[19] But the book did not appear until 1937, after Marquand's first major novel had become a bestseller. The author concurred with his publisher that book editions of his serials, both the Moto stories and Marquand's other works,[20] were bound to detract from his new stature as a serious writer. That the Moto stories became an exception to the decision against book versions of his serials reflected sales figures that were respectable enough to overcome McIntyre's misgivings. His firm would not regret its commitment. In the debate over the magazine serials in general and whether they should appear as books, the issues focused on literary merit and market potential for hardcover editions, but no one foresaw the paperback revolution and the volume of separate sales it would provide. *Think Fast, Mr. Moto* illustrates how the new format benefitted both the author and Little, Brown and Company. Two comparisons are significant. *The Late George Apley* sold 32,700 hardbound copies by the end of 1937; *Think Fast, Mr. Moto* had only 4,354 such sales from 1937 to 1972. But during those same thirty-five years it sold 848,000 paperback copies in a number of wartime and postwar editions.[21] Like all the other Moto books it was reissued in the mid-1980s and remains in print. The paperback sales undoubtedly reflect the popularity of the film series, which reached a huge international audience.

Although the story's premise involves northern China's political turmoil, the action centers on professional gambling and business corruption. The plotting shows signs of Marquand's hasty work; little exacting preparation was undertaken or needed. *Think Fast, Mr. Moto* moves quickly from an opening in Shanghai to its principal setting in the Hawaiian Islands. Since the narrative never demands geographic detail, Marquand could rely upon broad impressions from his residence and visits there during the 1930s, creating atmosphere through key words and images. Nor does the plot turn upon procedures in gambling or banking that required careful checking or explaining. It is a story that could be outlined and completed quickly. A fairly close summary of the narrative is nevertheless needed, however, since the material was substantially altered for the film version.

In the two opening chapters the parallel threads that later become joined are quickly introduced. One involves a proud American family's annoyance that a relative runs a gambling house near Honolulu; the other concerns secret financing of anti-Japanese activity in the new puppet state of Manchukuo. Hitchings Brothers is an old and respected American financial firm operating in the Far East; Wilson Hitchings has recently arrived in Shanghai to learn the business from his uncle William. The family has long been embarrassed because a distant relative, Ned Hitchings, had squandered his money and turned his home, Hitchings Plantation, into a popular casino now run by his daughter, Eva Hitchings, who refuses to sell out because she resents the family for having refused to help her father. Wilson Hitchings is now ordered to Hawaii to buy and close Hitchings Plantation. Before he leaves, a small Japanese man calls at his uncle's office. Moto inquires after a man named Chang Lo-shih, who had business ties in Manchuria before the change of control, but Hitchings denies all knowledge of Chang. He tells his nephew afterward that the caller is a Japanese agent using a subtle means to warn him against involvement. Wilson soon discovers his uncle does indeed deal with Chang. His curiosity is also aroused by what he is able to learn about the casino: the names of a Soviet citizen called Sergi and a Mr. Moto are mentioned to him.

Having thus fused his two basic ideas, Marquand shifts the locale to Hawaii, where the plot unfolds slowly. Wilson learns that the firm's local representative, Joe Wilkie, likes and sympathizes with Eva. The hero therefore realizes he must proceed alone—despite an anonymous note warning him against meddling. When he visits the casino, a somewhat neglected structure still tastefully furnished, he admits to being impressed: the girl is beautiful and capable, introducing the prospect of romance, but the gambling is a professional operation, suggesting the presence of gangsters. Paul Maddock, a gangster, indeed seems to run Hitchings Plantation. Then Moto appears in Eva's office. When a shot is fired through an open window the danger intensifies various fears: Wilson and Eva suspect each other of criminal associations—hers with ruthless gamblers and his with foreign agents; Moto feels threatened both by old adversaries and by the young Americans; Wilkie and Maddock also seem to be deeply involved—just how is kept in doubt by the author. Yet readers' uncertainties about roles and loyalties are exacerbated by successive incidents and maneuvers.

A curious point of the story is the author's improbable explanation of how his plot lines interconnect. Chang and others are supposedly sending money to Manchukuo for anti-Japanese activity by using an involved conduit through Hawaii. Funds destined for Manchukuo are forwarded to Hitchings Brothers' branch in the islands, withdrawn for movement across the casino tables by arranged losses and winnings, and smuggled out by Soviet and Chinese agents aboard freighters with friendly captains. The method seems extraordinarily complicated and contrived given the other options available. Its invention to link international intrigue in Manchukuo with a gambling operation in Honolulu shows more imagination than logic and plausibility.

The denouement comes slowly and without surprises. Maddock admits to Wilson that he muscled in on Eva's business, welcoming added payoffs for allowing the money transfers. But now he fears that Moto's presence will provoke the Soviets and Chinese. Learning from the gangster about another shipment of funds going out that night, Wilson again approaches Wilkie, who promises to check company records but moves to isolate the young couple. He wants to protect the girl and to conceal his own involvement. The couple are sent on a luncheon cruise aboard his boat, supposedly to talk out their differences, but are kept at sea by a pre-arranged engine breakdown. Cutting much of the overlong episode that follows would have been wise. The scene serves only as a conventional device: isolation of the hero so that he can demonstrate hidden resources as he faces his adversaries alone. Wilson has actually disarmed and tied up all three crew members before the couple discovers Moto: the Japanese cabin boy has told him the Americans will be at sea and has smuggled Moto aboard. After the crew free themselves, the two men must resubdue them. In the struggle Moto breaks the captain's arm and is then not averse to pressing it to make him talk. He also fixes the diesel engine in another display of his extraordinary talents. Meanwhile the couple reach an understanding as the girl explains she had to sell out and then front for Maddock temporarily.

At this point Wilson and Moto work at odds. The American wants the money shipped out, following the usual procedure of having Wilkie's boat meet an outbound freighter, so that no scandal will occur in Hawaii to hurt his family's business or Eva. Moto seeks to prevent the funds from leaving Hawaii. Eva tells only Wilson that the man in a photograph Moto showed the captain is the courier and probably a Soviet. Wilson conceals from Moto that Chang has reached Hawaii. Wilson, Eva, and Moto are all taken prisoner at the casino by Chang, Wilkie, Maddock, and their henchmen. Sergi and Chang depart with $200,000; Maddock goes outside under orders to kill Moto; Wilkie guards both Wilson and Eva. But Moto reappears to say he has agreed to let Maddock keep the money in return for killing Sergi and Chang at sea; his men have already seized Wilkie's boat and will now take it instead to a waiting Japanese freighter. Wilson and Moto quickly agree to suppress everything to protect the Hitchingses and Japan. The hero also requires Wilkie, who had become involved over personal debts, first to return the plantation, then to quit the firm within three months. Such a resolution shows the hero to be reasonable in the justice that he cannot leave to the authorities. Yet it also sidesteps the point that Japanese agents were operating on American territory and that he concealed such knowledge.

Think Fast, Mr. Moto was the first of the Moto films to be released by Twentieth Century–Fox. Although the film version will be discussed more fully later, it is helpful to summarize here the major changes made in characterizaton and plot, for they set the pattern for the entire film series. The motion picture presents Moto as a San Francisco importer and amateur detective trying to uncover a gang of smugglers; nearly all of the intrigue and action take place aboard a ship carrying Moto to Shanghai for his investigative triumph. Wilson Hitchings has become the heir of a shipping tycoon and been humanized as plain Bob Hitchings. Gone from the film are Soviet schemes involving Manchuria and Moto's role as a Japanese agent out to thwart them. Nor is there a gambling house in Hawaii where funds are being passed secretly. The screenplay offers a formula crime story with Moto substituted for Charlie Chan as the polite Oriental sleuth with neither nationalist feelings nor political aims. That the author's third adventure became the basis of the first film probably reflects the relative ease with which this particular story could be adapted to conform to just that noncontroversial content insisted upon by the producers. Hollywood continued the same approach through nearly all the films, despite the differences obvious to any reader of the stories turned out by Marquand. The filmmakers clearly wanted entertainment without complications. After only two productions they ignored the author's texts altogether and had screenwriters develop entirely new stories.

Moto made no further appearance in magazine serialization until midsummer 1938. The twenty-month gap between the conclusion of *Think Fast, Mr. Moto* in October 1936 and the beginning of *Mr. Moto Is So Sorry* in July 1938 is explained primarily by the author's busy schedule. During 1936 and 1937 he had completed final tasks connected with *The Late George Apley* and basked in his success leading to the Pulitzer Prize. Phenomenal sales and critical recognition also bolstered the arguments of those pressing the writer to concentrate on solid works: Adelaide too now strenuously opposed her new husband's further involvement with Moto. Still another possible complication to continuing the adventure series had arisen with Japan's invasion of China proper in July 1937 and the obvious uncertainty about how to handle the new military situation. Would American editors and readers still welcome tales about even a polite and rather likable Japanese agent? Yet there were reassuring signs as well. The two films in the series, retaining the author's titles but adapting his material, had done well in the theaters. But most important was the writer's own decision, for whatever combination of reasons, to proceed with the popular and lucrative series. Marquand soon devised a plot that avoided direct political traps and completed the manuscript by early 1938. Perhaps its apologetic title, *Mr. Moto Is So Sorry,* nevertheless had double meaning: it seems to suggest the agent's regrets about the course of recent events. The fourth adventure was quickly sold to the *Saturday Evening Post,* and McIntyre raised no objection to a book contract.[22] He may have thought a new Moto book would no longer hurt its author's reputation quite so much and that Marquand's fame might even help to boost sales. The *Saturday Evening Post* ran *Mr. Moto Is So Sorry* in seven parts from 2 July through 13 August 1938.[23]

Marquand set the story in the remote areas of northern China and based it heavily on his travels there in 1934. Two qualities stand out in the work. One is the particularly strong ring of authenticity evident in the descriptions and details, something readers perhaps sensed only vaguely at first, because of the other quality, the exciting momentum of the narrative that holds their attention. Frequent changes of scene as the principal characters make a long journey by train and then into the interior, combined with a melodramatic plot involving competing agents all concerned about a vital message being delivered, give the work more the flavor of the genuine thriller than any of the previous stories had achieved. Marquand avoided the touchy problems behind the contemporary headlines in part by making his hero a politically indifferent American. But since the real conflict is clearly between Moto and the intelligence service of the Soviet Union, he also made it possible for American readers to choose the former over the latter. Moto appears as a man of reason whose goal is to avoid escalation of the war in China. Thus the readers who distrusted communism and opposed war could find at least something to admire in the efforts of the polite title character.

The opening chapter introduces all the elements needed to gain and hold a reader's interest. Moto meets Calvin Gates aboard a small ship going from Japan to Japanese-controlled Korea. Gates had spent less than a week in Japan but the police were suspicious of the American. Gates calls himself an anthropology student en route to join the Gilbreth expedition at Ghuru Nor in Inner Mongolia, a border principality of great strategic importance. He seems not to know an American woman named Sylvia Dillaway traveling with a Soviet guide named Boris, even though she has claimed the same destination. Moto suspects both of being agents meddling in northern China. He thinks their apparent coolness once they meet is merely pretense, for he knows the Soviet is a key agent, and he is tracking a message the man is carrying. Japan hopes to bring Ghuru Nor under its control but fears antagonizing the Soviets and their puppets in Mongolia. When Boris spots Moto traveling the same route, he tells the woman he cannot accompany her all the way, only to Mukden, before they reach the Chinese frontier. He offers her a cigarette case as a parting gift. The case has an inlay of birds and reeds but appears to be typical workmanship and not valuable. Then during the layover at Mukden he visits Gates at his hotel, asking him to retrieve the case and deliver it to a friend. Boris is suddenly shot to death as Gates looks on helplessly. The chapter ends as Moto enters the room.

Various types of misunderstandings, mutual suspicions, and revelations complicate matters. At least one situation strains the reader's sense of plausibility. Gates has been raised by a wealthy uncle whose daughter, quite taken with Gilbreth and eager to help him, has forged her father's name on a check for $10,000. The young man has taken the blame upon himself and, thinking the police want him, is hurrying to ask the scientist to support his story. Portraying an intelligent thirty-two-year-old man, however chivalrous he might be, as behaving in such a manner, and not using cable communications, is a rather striking weakness in the plot. Of course Gilbreth has suspected the forgery, and Gates's uncle has covered for his daughter. Surely Marquand could have found a less flimsy motivation for Gates's journey. Other means designed to keep the plot moving smoothly are more believable. Moto helps conceal the murder, although his reason for wanting the cigarette case to continue on its way remains unclear. He becomes worried when told it has been stolen from the girl, who actually has given it to Gates. Because Moto suspects the theft story is a trick, Gates is removed from the train and searched at a station beyond Mukden, the Japanese confirming he indeed has the case. A Japanese colonel even gives him a gun thinking he works for Moto. At the Chinese border an Australian named Sam Hamby joins Dillaway and says he is adviser to Prince Wu Feng of Ghuru Nor and will see her to Gilbreth in Inner Mongolia. Hamby tries various means to get the case from Gates and finally convinces the girl that Gates must work for Moto. The young man, not knowing what is at stake or who is on which side, trusts no one.

Hamby explains to the girl that they cannot stop in Peking because unrest may soon close the rail line to Kalgan. Gates is seized as he leaves the crowded station in Peking and taken to a military camp for questioning by Major Ahara. He too wants the case. But incredibly no one has even searched Gates, who shoots a guard with his gun. Ahara begs Gates to kill him as well, knowing his carelessness leaves him without honor. The hero naturally refuses. Once again Moto appears and helps Gates get away. When the agent shows disappointment that Hamby does not have the case, Gates is more puzzled than ever by Moto, who finally explains that he wants the Soviets to receive the message. Thus the suspicion arises that the information is false. Moto takes Gates by plane over the mountains to reach Kalgan before the train carrying Hamby and Dillaway. Hamby is expected to stay at a compound owned by a rich trader named Holtz. Following Moto's instructions, the American reluctantly agrees to go to Holtz's place, tell everyone he is tired of taking Moto's orders and has left him alone at the hotel, and describe how Gates has seen Moto intimidate even the Japanese army. He must make clear Moto's power to control events. Nearly all of the characters—Gates, Dillaway, Gilbreth, Hamby, Wu Feng, and Ahara—are at the compound. In answer to Hamby's demand for the case, Dillaway has given him her own, which is similar; now Gates memorizes the design from the right case, destroying it when no one is watching. Hamby has also fallen for the ruse, and his men bring in the easily captured Moto. One additional person is present, the regional head of Soviet military intelligence, General Spirov, who turns out to be Boris's brother and a respected old adversary.

The denouement comes in the seventh and final chapter. Spirov's close questioning of Gates convinces him that his brother died as related and explains how Boris's cigarette case got to Kalgan. Realizing his isolation in the many-sided competition, Ahara bolts and is killed in the courtyard by Hamby, who remains confident of his strong bargaining position. But then Moto reveals why the message must reach the Soviet government: it tells enough about the Japanese military timetable in northern China to force a major policy decision. Will Moscow take action to stop the Japanese threat? Each intelligence chief feels the wrong answer will destroy his career, making suicide inevitable given his situation, and they all respect each other's professionalism and understanding of the stakes. Hamby's negotiations for the prince fail when he produces the wrong case, whereupon Gates speaks up, saying he can reproduce the design if both sides free all Americans. Moto and Spirov agree, the girl sketches the pattern as the young man describes it, and Holtz radios Moscow. When an answer comes back rather quickly, Moto thinks he has lost and asks Gates to see a certain gentleman in Tokyo, assuring him the agent has done his best. But instead Moscow reports the arrest and purging of many of Spirov's closest associates. Marquand thus made effective use of the contemporary news reports about the arrests and executions ordered by Stalin. With no military action expected, and his loyalty now suspect, the disgraced general shoots himself. Thus Ghuru Nor will fall without trouble under Japanese protection. Moto speaks quietly to the now helpless prince, whose guards take Hamby out to the courtyard, where he is shot for having killed Ahara. But Holtz may continue in business if he handles Japanese goods. The young couple plan to return home together. At the story's end the ever-civilized Moto asks that tea be served to everyone.

Marquand clearly chose to vary the types of situations and formats he devised for his tales featuring Moto. Highly significant in the concept and plotting of *Mr. Moto Is So Sorry* is his return to a strong espionage theme. He also reverted to the pattern of action and movement present in the first story but largely absent from its successors. Hence the fourth appearance of the agent, in terms of intrigue, excitement, and pacing of events, is a more traditional adventure yarn. Its special fascination, perhaps as travelogue more than mystery, stems from the realism of setting and detail the author could achieve through using his own experiences and records, first reconstructing his unusual train journey, then recalling people. Originals of both the prince and the merchant are to be found in people the author had met a few years earlier. But even though variations in both story type and plot situations had already occurred, the last prewar adventure of the wily agent differed substantially from its four predecessors, world conditions having forced some major rethinking if the series were to be viable.

Toward the end of 1940 Marquand wrote *Last Laugh, Mr. Moto* at his agent's urging. The manuscript of *H. M. Pulham, Esquire* had by then been completed for publication by Little, Brown and Company the following year. After Brandt argued that international conditions afforded an opportunity for a somewhat different type of Moto adventure, he and the author discussed story possibilities that would be less risky than previous plots, with Marquand warming to the idea of a tale about a secret weapon vital to America's security. European powers as well as Moto would be acting against America. Although such a story would probably require a setting other than the Far East, the shift in locale might pose no great problem, Hollywood films having already shown the title character operating elsewhere around the globe. Headlines about hemisphere security suggested the Caribbean as a likely and realistic battleground. Marquand nevertheless later expressed some discomfort over this last prewar Moto. Most of his feelings apparently stemmed from returning to a type of writing he wished to limit—particularly if he had misgivings about the timeliness or rightness of the project—and not from tackling the touchy and fluid international issues of the period, for he certainly never shared his second wife's rather isolationist political views or sympathized with her activities. Brandt knew how much the author enjoyed plotting and writing his adventure tales, however, and perhaps also felt he welcomed a change after the serious work of 1940. Yet the agent's motives may have been mercenary, as his rivals for influence over the author have claimed. For whatever motive, Marquand proceeded with the manuscript for Brandt, finishing on schedule.

A number of problems arose when it came to getting the work published. Rapidly shifting international conditions made everyone apprehensive about a tale involving the agent of an increasingly hostile nation. Editors at the *Saturday Evening Post* and *Ladies' Home Journal* both refused purchase.[24] Then *Collier's* agreed to a serialization under a title not using Moto's name: the story thus appeared as *Mercator Island* over eight weeks in September and October 1941 but aroused no reader furor. The cover of the issue with the first installment carried a prominent announcement—"John P. Marquand's New Novel—Mercator Island"—but made no mention of either the famous character or previous series. Readers might well have thought they were getting a preview or abridgment of his latest social satire. *Collier's* nevertheless gave the story the lead position for fiction and included a subheading identifying it with Moto: "Beginning the Caribbean adventures of the incredible Mr. Moto and the romance of the man and the girl who opposed his schemes." A three-quarter-page color illustration by Elmore Brown showed Moto wearing horn-rimmed glasses and looking quite young.[25]

The question of book publication meanwhile had renewed disagreement between writer and agent, the former resisting the idea, the latter stressing how much a book contract would earn in additional income. Marquand once more gave in to Brandt. Little, Brown and Company then nearly canceled the project after the Japanese attack on Pearl Harbor. But the 1942 book sales surprised everyone by surpassing those of any previous Moto novel.[26] The title of the book, *Last Laugh, Mr. Moto*, may well have helped sales, conveying to an angry American public that the Japanese agent had been outwitted, but conditions coming with World War II also encouraged light reading.

Marquand's remarks concerning this last story in the original grouping reflected the competing pressures he experienced with respect to Moto. But his words seem to belie his actions. He told McIntyre he considered the work a minor effort undertaken only to provide Brandt with income, neither the project nor the money meaning much to him personally, and Marquand assured the publisher that there would be no subsequent book version regardless of Brandt's urging.[27] He claimed his agent had "the most amazing attitude about book publication. He seems to feel that a publishing house is a kind of sausage machine to which the author-agent throws a lot of manuscripts, the use of which has been exhausted elsewhere."[28] But even after Marquand had indeed succumbed to Brandt's views, and the material was in McIntyre's hands for a book edition, he insisted to McIntyre that the Moto work was unimportant: "Between you and me it is a completely perfunctory piece of work. While I might devote a day to making a few minor changes your suggestion that I build up Mr. Moto by a few adroit additions would take more time than the project is worth."[29] Some who knew Marquand and his family situation have detected the arguments of Adelaide in such remarks.[30] Not only did her old opposition to what she considered unworthy projects continue, perhaps gaining headway at this time when she was expecting their second child, but even the assertion that the money did not mattter expressed her outlook. Pleasing his wife was perhaps only one reason for the novelist's petulance with respect to the work. Marquand also felt increased anger over developments in the Pacific. He had long followed events in the Far East closely, disliking Japan's aggressions, and the attack on Pearl Harbor had upset him greatly.[31] Marquand was understandably touchy about his Japanese agent during the time of Pearl Harbor.

As the story opens, Bob Bolles recalls events that began in November 1940 at Kingston, Jamaica, when he chartered his schooner, *Thistlewood*, to a young New York couple named Kingman for a leisurely pleasure cruise. Early in the narrative the author piques reader interest by dropping various hints of mystery and trouble: I. A. Moto keeps a shop in Kingston selling Japanese goods; Malcolm (Mac) and Helen Kingman seem to have difficulty with Americanisms; Mac calls his wife both Helen and Hélène; Bolles says he knows Kingman will kill him after a bridge game; an American destroyer called the *Smedley* puts in at Kingston on some unknown mission; a man named Charles Durant claiming to be a wine dealer from Portugal has inquired about Kingman; Moto and several others have all visited a place called Mercator Island. Bolles himself is a former navy flier who quit in a huff over a lost promotion and then spent two years as a drifter and quarrelsome drunk and is now no longer welcome in Jamaica. Inspector Jameson's order to leave in fact forces him to take the charter from Kingman. He even accepts the man's explanation that his interest in little-known Mercator Island and its long-abandoned sugar plantation came from reading an old book. But he refuses a request from Captain Burke of the *Smedley* to help the American navy search the Caribbean because he knows its lesser islands. Burke tells him that the Germans have sunk a French freighter carrying a crated airplane with a special American part, but survivors reveal that the ship's captain had already hidden the valuable cargo on some unknown island. Now European agents, the American navy, and perhaps even Japanese spies are all seeking likely Carribbean islands. But Bolles is still too embittered to help Burke search.

Out at sea tension builds. Bolles learns from Tom, his Jamaican crewman, that Moto has tried to discover their destination; Helen Kingman and Bolles are attracted to each other but he spots her errors about New York and America; she eventually admits she is French but continues to seem edgy; Tom also senses something is wrong and reports the disappearance of all weapons kept on the *Thistlewood*; the Kingmans' supposedly Swedish valet, Oscar, speaks German and knows boats well. By the time they reach Mercator Island the hero realizes the Kingmans are not married, that they want the airplane part Burke has told him about, and that Kingman still needs him only because Oscar does not know navigation.

On the island they find a fisherman's shelter made from wood bearing words identifying it as the crating. Then Moto appears. He has taken a fast cruiser from Kingston because he also wants the special device, having already tried in vain to penetrate the American factory where it was being produced. The Japanese agent reminds Kingman they have previously met in Vladivostok and Berlin, shocking Helen into realizing that Kingman is a professional only hired by the French and now betraying French interests. Moto and Kingman join forces when Moto reports the *Smedley* is coming. Helen wants the part to help France; Bolles seeks to preserve its secret for America; Kingman hopes to sell it to Germany. At this point Jameson also reveals himself and says he came concealed on Moto's chartered cruiser. His suspicions were aroused when a Japanese shopkeeper hired a very fast boat. He also reports that Oscar is wanted by authorities in Jamaica for strangling Durant, who Helen knows was a French agent, but Jameson is soon overpowered, leaving Kingman and Oscar in apparent control. A cautious alliance uniting Helen, Moto, and Bolles has nevertheless been forming. But everyone is stuck on the island: Tom holds the schooner at sea awaiting a signal, and Jameson has sent the cruiser back to bring help from Jamaica.

When the fuselage is finally found, Helen tells the others the special part is a new turbo supercharger, something that even Moto appears to accept, but a panel switch for a night tracking instrument quickly interests Bolles, who decides not to say anything. Kingman wants to kill Bolles, but he still needs the schooner, so they pass time playing bridge, as Bolles had predicted in chapter 1. Shortly afterward the rivalry is resolved violently: Oscar's attempt to strangle Bolles backfires and his own skull is crushed during the struggle, and Kingman only wounds Moto before his agile opponent shoots him to death. Bolles destroys both the supercharger and the beaming device before reappearing to confront Moto. He learns that Moto and Helen had been planning to kill Oscar and Kingman even before the flight. Moto is pleased to see him alive but admits he would not have risked his mission to stop anyone from disposing of Bolles.

As they await daylight so that Tom can bring the schooner through the shallows, Helen looks after the wounded Moto. Then she and Bolles go off quietly to discuss their future lives. Helen feels she must continue her intelligence work but agrees to talk further en route to Kingston; Bolles has regained his sense of duty and self-respect through their experience and meeting Helen. Moto has brought a radio and has summoned a plane to pick him up; Jameson will be rescued by the British; the others must be gone before the arrival of police or the *Smedley*. But Moto becomes especially eager for the *Thistlewood's* departure. As the couple leaves in the dinghy Moto draws a gun, says he knew the real prize was a night combat device, and gloats that "Beam 21 A" will now be his alone. Unaware the part has been smashed, he thinks he has the last laugh, but triumph belongs to the couple.

Most noteworthy in this story are the shift in locale and the out-witting of the famous agent. The former was perhaps unnecessary and certainly unfortunate. A suitable plot and site using the Far East might well have been developed, but Marquand had not been deeply interested in this Moto project, as his remarks to McIntyre about book publication and revision had made clear. And although the relocation avoided difficulties posed by the rapidly changing Asian situation, given the inevitable time lapse between writing and final appearance in print, the Caribbean setting lacked the previous stories' rich background color and detail. Marquand's limited firsthand knowledge of the new locale simply caused him to develop a plot not requiring specific information about the Caribbean. Moto's failure was a requisite plot twist, however, considering popular attitudes in the early 1940s. Americans might nevertheless be upset to realize the extensive intelligence operations attributed to Japan: Moto had once again called upon local agents in place to aid him and had admitted to having spied inside America.

Problems marketing *Last Laugh, Mr. Moto,* combined with Marquand's ambivalence toward the series even before the Pearl Harbor attack, led him to discontinue the Mr. Moto stories. Moto would nevertheless be revived fifteen years later when personal and world conditions had changed.

The special circumstances leading to creation of the last Moto novel in the mid-1950s were remarkably like those in the mid-1930s, when the first Moto story had helped the author escape marital problems. Adelaide would not accept her marriage's failure and now steadfastly refused to divorce Marquand. Once again the *Saturday Evening Post* made an offer: Stuart Rose suggested that Marquand revive the Moto character and proposed a $75,000 advance with $5,000 for travel to the Far East.[32] Marquand seized the opportunity and began a world tour with his oldest son in late June 1955. The first part took him to many places—Honolulu, Tokyo, Hong Kong, Singapore, Bangkok, Cambodia, Colombo, Beirut, Cairo—but lasted little more than a month. Marquand had arranged to meet Carol Brandt at Lake Como in early August, and from there they went to Paris and then to a suburban hotel, with Marquand dictating the Moto story to Carol during their stay in Versailles.[33] The collaboration recalls how she had typed his first story in the series over twenty years earlier. Meanwhile Carl Brandt worked on business aspects of the project in his New York office.

Much is known about the author's feelings concerning the book. Carol Brandt remembered the pleasure both felt in Versailles: "John was doing what he liked to do best of all, writing, and I was there with him in a pleasant place, helping get his book down on paper." Her husband assured the *Saturday Evening Post*'s Rose toward late August that work in France was proceeding well: "John has a good story, subtle and adult as well as strong and deadly, timely and knowledgeable. It will be laid in Tokyo and Cambodia." He wrote the author to say he and Rose both looked forward to reading the manuscript.[34] In September Marquand and Carol continued their work at Claridge's Hotel in London. She recalled:

> Everything that John wrote he wrote with enormous joy—that was to me one of the special things about his writing, that he never wrote about anything he disliked—but this Mr. Moto book was a special joy for him because it was returning to an old character he had always loved, and applying to it all the skills and subtleties he had acquired since the last Moto. The book just zipped along, with John loving every minute of it. You could tell how much John enjoyed what he was doing by watching the expression on his face. As he dictated, his upper lip and mustache would curl with pleasure. It was wonderful to watch a man get such a kick out of his own words and sentences.[35]

He completed a first draft in a little more than six weeks and made revisions into the autumn. In November he wrote to one of his sons about the 90,000-word manuscript: "It may not be art but it is not bad cabinetmaking."[36] Marquand elaborated his point during an interview for *Newsweek:*

> I revived Mr. Moto for my amusement. It didn't take too long to write. I wanted to see whether or not I was still able to write a mystery, one of the most interesting forms of literary craftsmanship, if not art, that exists. I like to think that it is better than my early mystery stories; it ought to be, because I am twenty years older.[37]

Clearly the author felt pleased with his results.

Editors at the *Saturday Evening Post* did not agree. In particular they disliked the story's unhappy ending, one the author felt could not be altered without damaging the realism of the account, so that he rejected their request to change it. Marquand resented what he saw as being treated like a staff writer on assignment who had to please his editor. As he explained, "For some reason, literary hack though I am, the frayed vestiges of my artistic integrity made me refuse to make the change."[38] Although his self-disparagement was overdone, the decision was correct, for alteration would have been unfortunate. Yet he rather characteristically chose to forget or overlook the big advance and travel funds he had accepted. The *Saturday Evening Post* soon conceded and ran *Rendezvous in Tokyo* in eight installments from November 1956 to the middle of January 1957.[39] Marquand's name with the words "A New Novel" shared the cover announcement with another item, but no mention was made of Marquand's story title or of Moto. A heading at the start of the initial segment clarified the situation: "One of fiction's favorite sleuths of all time, the inscrutable Mr. Moto, reappears at last in this exciting adventure by an eminent and versatile American." The piece received the lead position in the issue, and William A. Smith provided illustrations that stressed romance rather than the spy theme. Also included toward the back of the magazine was an interview with the author in which he discussed his writing methods and decision to revive the character.[40]

Little, Brown and Company agreed to the title chosen by Marquand and brought out the book as *Stopover: Tokyo*. Yet the magazine's title was more aptly worded, the city being a destination rather than a layover point, and underscored the story's element of romance. It is worth noting about both titles, however, that neither referred to the famous character. An even more extraordinary omission would occur when the novel was made into a film. Despite the sometimes unfavorable reviews, especially from admirers of the writer's major novels who took this work much too seriously, the book became a bestseller. *Stopover: Tokyo*'s sales benefitted particularly from its selection for members of the Book-of-the-Month Club.[41] Readers obviously welcomed a new adventure of a familar old figure even if some critics showed dismay. Carol Brandt meanwhile had acted for her ill husband in selling the film rights in Hollywood. Twentieth Century–Fox agreed to an advantageous contract with a base payment of $65,000.[42]

The story line relied on contemporary events. Jack Rhyce is an experienced American intelligence agent in his mid-thirties starting an assignment in Japan to investigate the Asia Friendship League. He was chosen because he knows Japanese from a childhood in Japan and from studies at a language school. Using a carefully arranged cover as an educator evaluating the group's activities for one of its benefactors, Rhyce will help a fellow agent, Bill Gibson, the service's local man in Tokyo, who has reported surges in Communist agitation and now fears some assassination to provoke mass demonstrations. Washington thinks the mastermind may be an American Communist known as Ben Bushman and often referred to as "Big Ben." Bushman's superior may be a Soviet named Skirov who has frequently visited Japan. Suspense is introduced by incidents in San Francisco, where Rhyce finds out that Ruth Bogart has been assigned as his partner. In public they must appear to be lovers. But soon they realize they are being watched—encountering first a young Japanese man who urges that his uncle in Tokyo be their local guide, and then hearing lines from an old operetta called *The Red Mill* sung softly by a retreating eavesdropper—although they are not yet unduly alarmed. During a refueling stop at Wake Island they hear another tune from the show and meet the big American who has been singing it: Bushman is thought to have experience in amateur theatricals, and the couple conclude they have met "Big Ben." But they wonder if the Communists are also onto them.

Moto appears in chapter 5 to meet the Americans' plane in Tokyo. Now middle-aged with graying hair, he remains extremely courteous, but he is still given to peculiar clothing. He explains that his nephew has cabled him and arranges to rejoin the couple after they have rested. Rhyce contacts Gibson to report what has happened and to get information about Bushman and Moto. He becomes worried when Gibson points out that there are no Japanese names of just those syllables, making the man's identity and motives suspect, and when he realizes that Harry Pender in the Asia Friendship League's local office is a conspirator.

The scene then shifts to a "honeymoon" hotel in the mountains at Myakoshita where all the principals have gathered. After again hearing someone singing a *Red Mill* tune, the couple spot their acquaintance from Wake Island in the crowd at the hotel bar; he introduces himself as Ben Bushman, an airline flight engineer in Japan for layover about ten days each month. His attraction to Ruth is quite obvious. Later the couple find Gibson dead in his hotel bungalow, the death made to look accidental from alcohol and barbiturates, but Rhyce soon recognizes it as a professional killing. They know Bushman is responsible. Despite the growing love affair with Rhyce, which both know violates their training, Ruth must nevertheless encourage the killer's interest, for they cannot lose contact with him.

Moto reveals himself as a Japanese official when Rhyce is charged with Gibson's murder and identified as "Big Ben." He will put Ruth on a plane home if Rhyce will agree to talk, but threatens torture if necessary, his anger rising when Rhyce twice calls him a "little yellow bastard." The young Japanese man in San Francisco had reported Rhyce present when the unseen person sang a *Red Mill* tune, a nervous habit of "Big Ben's" Moto had already known about. Bushman himself has posed as an American intelligence agent to tell Moto that the man they both have been seeking is Rhyce. Once Moto and Rhyce overcome their misconceptions of each other, Moto expresses mortification at misidentifying "Big Ben," whom he has pursued without ever actually having seen him. Moto then reveals much about his personal and professional background in a long conversation with Rhyce. Agreeing to share knowledge and join efforts, Rhyce and Moto go after Pender and Bushman, the action shifting back to the capital. Moto believes the conspirators will try to kill a liberal politician and blame the Americans. Bushman soon telephones Ruth. Despite misgivings about her undertaking such a dangerous task, Rhyce and Moto let her arrange to meet Bushman on the Ginza, where they plan to seize him when he arrives. But she is abducted from the hotel before she can leave for the appointment.

All pretenses end when Pender telephones Rhyce to strike a deal; in verifying her capture, Ruth warns Rhyce against any compromise. As professionals they know she will be tortured and killed by the Communists. Their cover had held longer than they had expected, until the visiting Skirov recognized Rhyce from a Moscow incident years before, alerting the others to his real identity. Until then they were regarded as innocents and dupes. But Rhyce has heard Pender mention a respected Japanese politician who Moto agrees must be Bushman's target. Moto immediately arranges to pose as the victim, replacing household servants with his own men, but leaving first crack at the killer to Rhyce. With Bushman himself the assassin, the two antagonists engage in a desperate fight until Moto feels he must intervene, giving the Communist to his men for interrogation. Moto lets Rhyce avoid responsibility for what will happen but assures him that his men are "very conscientious." With warm respect for each other they go to the Asia Friendship League's office and find Pender and Skirov waiting for word that their scheme has begun with success.

The final chapter finds Rhyce back in Washington reporting to his superior. Skirov has fallen eight stories; his death was never explained, but his fingerprints were verified by Moto. Pender is taken away for questioning and, according to newspapers, dies in a traffic mishap in Tokyo. The unknown fate of Bushman and deaths of Skirov and Pender again show that Moto can be quite ruthless. But the "Chief" wonders why he never encountered Moto during his own intelligence work in the Orient before the war and observes also that Moto is merely a suffix in Japanese names. Rhyce suggests Moto might have been abroad when the "Chief" was on Asian duty, and he is undoubtedly important enough now to stay generally behind the scenes. Rhyce promises the "Chief" to record his impressions of Moto for Washington.

Marquand had every justification for being pleased with the last adventure of Moto. The book is by far the best of of the entire series, allowing the series to conclude with dignity; the writer had sensed how the genre itself needed to be changed. He caught the mood of the postwar world, one beset by cold-war tensions and struggles, and noted how moral lines had become blurred. For the first time he made the American hero a professional agent, portraying him as disillusioned by his work in intelligence, and let an American heroine die in a horrible but unstated way. Marquand also gave insights to the values that shaped Moto. All of his major characters are developed more subtly and realistically in this book than in earlier stories. With its often solemn tone and unexpectedly sombre ending, *Stopover: Tokyo* anticipates the kind of novels later written by John Le Carré, who typifies one strain in contemporary handling of such content. That the author was ahead of his time is clear not only from the magazine's initial but unsuccessful objections; evidence of similar reactions to his search for depth and realism in characterization and structuring is also found in reviews. One example is the writer who thought the genre should be kept simple: "Though the spy story may be filled with corpses, it is no place for either tragedy or revelation."[43] The filmmakers agreed: their screenplay removed the very features and strengths that give the novel its texture and impact.

Many patterns and dissimilarities among the five early and one postwar Moto stories can readily be discerned from these synopses of their contents. But separate discussions of key conceptual and literary elements are needed for full identification and explanation of the author's handling of his material. The next chapter therefore builds upon these plot summaries to examine in the series as a whole such matters as the treatment of story structure and characterization and the depiction of the intelligence milieu.

1. *Ming Yellow* ran in the *Saturday Evening Post* from 8 December 1934 through 12 January 1935. For the announcement see "Next Week" in the 1 December 1934 issue, p. 76. The magazine had also taken out full-page newspaper advertisements to publicize the serial.

2. Letter from McIntyre to Bernice Baumgarten at Brandt and Brandt, quoted in Bell, p. 226.

3. Ibid., quoting letter from Marquand to Roger Scaife.

4. Ibid., pp. 226–27.

5. Birmingham, pp. 67–68.

6. "Next Week," *Saturday Evening Post*, 23 March 1935, p. 120. Lorimer had been highly pleased with *Ming Yellow* and predicted *No Hero* would be a "second successive smashing hit." Bell, p. 226.

7. The exact dates are 30 March, 6, 13, 20, and 27 April, and 4 May 1935. It is impossible to explain why both Birmingham, p. 305, and Bell, p. 249, err in saying that *Mr. Moto Takes a Hand* was the title used in the serialization. That may have been a title given some later re-issue of the book in paperback.

8. *Saturday Evening Post*, 30 March 1935. Moto was rarely shown in the illustrations, which tended to stress romance, but he was portrayed as a smiling, round-faced man without glasses on one occasion. In the films Moto wore glasses, and many people assume the original Moto also used them. Ibid., 2 July 1938, p. 6.

9. Bell, p. 227.

10. Ibid., p. 229.

11. Ibid., p. 249.

12. *No Hero*, pp. 120–21.

13. See *Stopover: Tokyo*, pp. 73–80.

14. *No Hero*, pp. 162–63.

15. Bell, pp. 248–49.

16. Ibid., p. 249. The "Next Week" section in the issue of 1 February 1936 identified the serial as the major coming attraction, and Marquand's story got cover mention on 8 February. It was also the lead feature. *Thank You, Mr. Moto* appeared in the *Saturday Evening Post* on 8, 15, 22, and 29 February and 7 and 14 March 1936.

17. Letter from Adelaide to her mother, Blanche Ferry Hooker, 28 March 1936. Bell, p. 249.

18. See "Next Week" in the *Saturday Evening Post*, 5 September 1936, p. 92. The serial appeared in the issues dated 12, 19, and 26 September and 3, 10, and 17 October 1936.

19. Bell, p. 248.

20. Marquand was writing serials besides those featuring Moto. One in particular was affected by the decision against book editions. During spring 1937 the *Saturday Evening Post* ran a Civil War serial entitled *Eight-Three-Eight;* Marquand and McIntyre both felt a book version would hurt Marquand's stature after *The Late George Apley*'s success. Bell, pp. 255–56; Birmingham, pp. 123–25. But McIntyre accepted *Mr. Moto Is So Sorry* for

book publication on 21 February 1938 in a letter to Bernice Baumgarten. Bell, p. 256. That was months before the novel's magazine serialization.

21. Ibid., pp. 227, 255. During World War II *Think Fast, Mr. Moto* appeared in both Pocket Book and Mercury editions. Ibid., p. 347. Hardcover sales of all prewar Moto novels ranged from 3,000 to 5,000 copies a title. Hamburger, p. 6.

22. Bell, p. 256.

23. The *Saturday Evening Post* ran *Mr. Moto Is So Sorry* on 2, 9, 16, 23, and 30 July and 6 and 13 August 1938. See also "Next Week" in the 25 June 1938 issue, p. 88.

24. Bell, p. 220.

25. *Collier's* serialized *Mercator Island* on 6, 13, 20, and 27 September and 4, 11, 18, and 25 October 1941. See especially p. 11 of the 6 September issue. *Collier's* still sold for five cents in 1941. The magazine serialized another Marquand spy novel, *It's Loaded, Mr. Bauer,* in 1942. It deals with wartime espionage in South America but does not work well. The only book edition appeared in Britain. Marquand obviously did not give up writing spy adventures with his last prewar Moto work.

26. Bell, p. 220; Birmingham, p. 154.

27. Birmingham, pp. 153–54. Even after he got the author's oral agreement, Brandt was unsure of Marquand, fearing he would change his mind before signing.

28. Bell, p. 349.

29. Ibid., p. 501.

30. Birmingham, pp. 153–54.

31. Holman, p. 21.

32. Rose was an associate editor at the magazine. Such a large advance undoubtedly required high-level approval; the newsstand price for each issue was fifteen cents at the time. Birmingham, p. 266, asserts that Rose consciously repeated the magazine's offer and role of 1934.

33. Ibid., pp. 266–68; Bell, pp. 439, 447–49.

34. Birmingham, p. 268.

35. Ibid., pp. 268–69.

36. Bell, p. 455.

37. "Why Did Mr. Moto Disappear?" *Newsweek,* 21 January 1957, p. 106.

38. Bell, p. 455. See also Birmingham, pp. 270–71. Marquand vowed never again to undertake any commissioned writing.

39. The exact dates are 24 November, 1, 8, 15, 22, and 29 December 1956, and 5 and 12 January 1957. Announcement of the serial appeared in the issue a week before publication but lacked any special emphasis. See the *Saturday Evening Post,* 17 November 1956, p. 160.

40. Ibid., 24 November 1956, pp. 23, 24, 152.

41. Bell, p. 227. See also Birmingham, p. 270, regarding the book title.

42. Ibid., p. 271. The sale of the story rights to the studio was Carol Brandt's first major piece of business as the firm's acting head.

43. *Newsweek,* 21 January 1957, p. 106.

III

Marquand's Narratives: Methods and Patterns

ARQUAND NEVER CONSIDERED his many adventure novels
to be literature or art, but he appreciated keenly the
skills needed to create an intriguing mystery, everything
from conceiving a workable plot to monitoring the textual details, and
especially prided himself on his craftsmanship in the Moto stories.
That sense of satisfaction in what he called good "cabinetmaking" is
fully justified when the works themselves are scrutinized.

Magazine fiction in the interwar "golden age" of the big weekly publications adhered to conventions that Marquand had little difficulty in
mastering. He seemed to learn quickly how to combine the desired
elements—romance and adventure, attractive characters, conflict and
reconciliation—in variable arrangements set forth in a clear and con-
cise style. Friends had always admired his ability as a raconteur, hearing him turn simple occurrences into enjoyable anecdotes, and such
storytelling skills made writing come easily. He even came to dictate
the drafts of his work in order to capture the natural flow of narration.[1]
Story settings were far-ranging and often exotic—the boxing world,
France in World War I, New England, American generals, Hawaii, the
South Seas, China, the Civil War, South America, horse-racing
events—but repetitions were frequent given his substantial output.[2]
The need to introduce a new locale had indeed helped prompt the
original offer to send him abroad for fresh material. With his plots and
story structures also conforming to established patterns, and his prose
kept simple and straightforward for a large readership to enjoy with
little effort, success in the field of popular fiction might continue in-
definitely. Yet he obviously came to yearn for recognition as a serious
novelist, finding himself caught between old friends who had

promoted his early development and others who now wanted to rechannel his efforts, a conflict of directions and personalities the vacillating writer never fully escaped. The Moto stories form an important part of the struggle involving Marquand's career.

Three men who had long associations with Marquand helped shape his writing style and production. Since two of them were primarily interested in his work for magazines and the other sought to advance his stature as a major novelist, they worked at cross purposes during the later decades of Marquand's life. The continuing struggle placed a heavy burden on the author, who sometimes vented his irritation in harsh comments and actions, but he nevertheless owed a great debt to such mentors. His long apprenticeship as a writer of popular short stories and serialized novels gave him the directness and clarity of construction and expression that make his most serious novels accessible and enjoyable. But some literary critics, perhaps deceived by his lucid prose and conventional approach in a period when modernist tenets favored experimentation, found his work shallow. That charge, when leveled against his major novels, lacks merit. Yet his experience as a magazine writer conditioned him to adhere closely to editorial expectations and marketable formulas in much of his work. The guidance he received from his lifelong agent and earliest magazine editor never completely left his consciousness.

Carl Brandt began acting as Marquand's literary agent in the early 1920s and served him until Brandt died in 1957.[3] A highly skilled editor and astute negotiator, Brandt became both teacher and friend to Marquand, working energetically to advance the writer's career. Using his experience in the magazine field, he suggested story lines and settings, advised the author on improvements—especially insisting on more romance—edited and otherwise shaped his manuscripts, and helped determine the serial divisions. Brandt also got Marquand top prices for his work in the 1920s and 1930s.[4] Marquand later portrayed his agent and recreated their collaboration in a scene in *Wickford Point*: the successful commercial writer, Jim Calder, watches while his agent, George Stanhope, quickly doctors a manuscript. Brandt's enthusiasm and forcefulness repeatedly provided the necessary counterweights to the insecurity and frequent self-doubts of Marquand. Their friendship became especially important to the author during the difficult months when his first marriage was failing. Carol was similarly devoted to Marquand long before their affair; her help during summer 1934 greatly speeded the first Moto. Brandt's promotion of stock fiction that would be quickly salable to the popular magazines inevitably led to disagreements as the writer saw himself more and more as a serious novelist in the late 1930s.

Both during his lifetime and in later assessments many people blamed Brandt for Marquand's failure to abandon magazine writing and concentrate on major fiction. At issue was not only the continued production of lighter works but also the abridgment of some of his best novels for the high-paying slick magazines. As the author's literary agent, Brandt received a 10-percent commission on all sales, and some accused him of pushing serializations merely to increase his own income from Marquand's stories and novels.[5] Adelaide in particular objected to what she considered the money-grubbing approach taken by Brandt.[6] Yet as long as the author himself remained obsessed with making money, being willing to turn out a stream of popular fiction, his agent also had to handle another problem that is often overlooked. Any notion that Marquand continued to write light fiction for magazines only to free himself financially for his other works, a common misconception, was certain to annoy editors who might conclude he was not really committed to the material Brandt offered to them.[7] Brandt also dealt with representatives of Hollywood. Those who accuse the agent of venal motives tend to ignore the fact that the author himself seldom refused for long to cooperate in any endeavor designed to earn more money. Whatever blame is assessed cannot be as one-sided as the author's second wife and various friends liked to claim.

The influence of editor George Horace Lorimer of the *Saturday Evening Post* had also begun early.[8] Lorimer had first bought Marquand's work in the early 1920s, thereafter advising him on themes and stylistic matters and urging him to avoid any experimentation that might confuse readers, and Lorimer had financed the trip to Asia in 1934. That commitment showed a type of symbiosis that had by then developed: the young author had mastered what the powerful editor had taught him was wanted; the magazine came to depend upon the kind of fiction its popular writer produced. From 1922 to 1940 the magazine published nearly a hundred stories and about a dozen serials by Marquand. Only about ten of his works during that period went to other magazines.[9] Lorimer understandably expected the author to continue supplying the magazine with a steady flow of romantic adventures in the mid-1930s. In particular he wanted the intriguing Moto character to make more than one appearance. But at the same time he agreed with Marquand's agent that the projected "Boston novel" was not well suited for the magazine's readers.[10] Lorimer and Brandt together therefore exerted considerable pressure on the writer after his return from Asia in 1935. During that autumn Marquand wrote the second Moto story they wanted. Twentieth Century–Fox bought film rights to the first tale in October 1935. Brandt urged development of still further stories in late November: "I think you'll be an awful idiot if you don't let these things go [on]. It means things in motion pictures and it's very worthwhile."[11] When Marquand subsequently produced a third Moto adventure he was accommodating Lorimer and Brandt but postponing completion of the novel his second wife and McIntyre wanted. In addition to his desire for the income, and possible uncertainty about his ability to finish the serious novel as he envisioned it, the author recognized his obligation to the magazine. Lorimer's death in 1937 nevertheless released him from at least the personal bond that Lorimer had forged in 1921.

Chief among those who pressed Marquand after the success of *The Late George Apley* to limit himself to serious novels were Alfred McIntyre at Little, Brown and Company and the author's new wife. McIntyre had waged his campaign long before 1937.[12] For several years he had sought to get Marquand to finish his "Boston novel" but knew that Marquand's first marriage and divorce had left him unsettled. During that period travel and creation of adventure stories seemed to give the author more peace of mind than concentrated work on the novel. McIntyre remained patient and even published the books featuring Moto. At the same time he resisted book versions of the author's other magazine serials and opposed bringing out collections of his short stories.[13] After the sales and critical success of *The Late George Apley* he wanted other serious novels to follow.[14] Yet it ought to be noted that book publishers as well as magazine editors guide authors to write the kinds of books they have found to be financially profitable. McIntyre certainly knew what he wanted from Marquand. Adelaide also argued that it would be regressive for her husband to return to popular fiction after winning a Pulitzer Prize.[15] Always a forceful advocate of her views, with influence extending by the early 1940s even to joint ownership of Marquand's new copyrights and thus royalty sharing,[16] she still could not control his decisions. Her approach may well have caused unexpected results. She undoubtedly failed to sense that her pressure produced the very discomfort that led him to seek escape in plotting and writing adventure tales. And Adelaide never realized that her husband's later career decisions were influenced by at least some degree of guilt arising from his long affair with Brandt's wife.

Marquand took considerable satisfaction in his consistent success as a magazine writer from the very outset of his career in the 1920s. "Unlike most young writers, I have had no early struggles. Seemingly I have always managed to write the sort of stories which the popular magazines demand, and I have sold everything I have been able to produce at unduly high prices."[17] Basic to such achievement was the purposefulness in his approach, for he launched and developed even his routine works with unusual care, taking genuine pride in applying his skills as a craftsman. "I can write on order—get a real kick out of doing adventure series—and when I'm doing a job whether on order or on my own I'm sure that it is good."[18] Marquand also voiced his attitude through his alter ego, Jim Calder, the defensive commercial writer who appears in *Wickford Point:* "We . . . took pride in our product, not the wild free pride of an artist, but the solid pride of a craftsman."[19] Friends repeatedly noticed how much pleasure the author always derived from his work and especially from putting together the action stories. Yet he never equated a quality product turned out for the mass market with a finely wrought novel that could be called literature. Such awareness and honesty sometimes led him to comment about his lighter works in terms that seem disparaging. But he was merely recognizing that popular fiction, however smoothly it might be executed, had to conform to basic formulas, rules, and patterns that robbed it of subtleties. Marquand expressed the same feeling in his later explanation of why he curtailed his output of Moto and other magazine adventures in the early 1940s: "I stopped because I wished to do something serious. I was tired of that literary form; it was all too easy."[20]

Those who knew him well realized how much Marquand worried about his image and what critics said. Comparison of two letters he wrote in spring 1939 with one written exactly six years later in 1945 show the conflicting sides of his self-concept. The earlier letters reflect a time when he was still producing popular fiction. In one he assured Brandt it would be "utter folly for me to sneer" at the kind of writing that had supported him for many years and added, "I have always been proud and pleased to be identified as a writer for the Post and I shall continue to be as long as they want to have me."[21] For a reader he elaborated his views a week later:

> I share the impatience which I imagine every contributor of the Post must feel toward the attitude of the intelligentsia about magazine fiction. The truth is that most of our solemn and sanctimonious artists in the short story haven't the technical skill to write for

the *Post* market, and the critics on the whole have the most abysmal ignorance of the kind of work that is being done there. I really feel that the backlog of any literature we have in America lies in the magazines. Granted a lot of the work there may be second-rate, it is technically very competent and it furnishes a real impetus for literature.[22]

But following his series of successful novels he wrote to a serviceman that he had at first been anxious to do what people told him, "and I know now that I fell into the hands of the worst possible instructors." He considered his quick success at the *Saturday Evening Post* to be unfortunate on balance: he had learned skills but not produced art.

I also found myself associated with a bright and high-powered literary agent. In my callowness I had the greatest respect for his opinion and consequently his influence upon me was enormous. It is only quite recently that I have realized that his mind was on nothing except commercial literary profits and that he never possessed the slightest artistic feeling and was almost wholly devoid of any literary background.[23]

Considering his substantial professional and personal debt to his agent, for whom he continued to profess friendship despite what he called occasionally bad literary advice, and who knew the author was sexually involved with his wife, such comments surpass simple ingratitude and smack of callousness and egocentrism. Marquand also withdrew book negotiation rights from Brandt and began handling them himself in the 1940s.[24] The agent continued to work out the magazine and film contracts, but there was little material for those media in the postwar years.[25]

A more mellow attitude prevailed in the early 1950s as Marquand again defended his background and wide interests. The occasion was publication of a collection of his short works, *Thirty Years*; his foreword provided a vehicle for reiterating his views. Directing most of his comments to short stories, which he considered the most difficult literary form, he maintained that conventions always resulted in formulae, and even prestige magazines imposed their own styles. But much of what he said applied to serialized novels as well. It was obvious that the old criticisms still rankled. But Marquand observed in reference to his slim output of magazine fiction in the 1940s that "I am still not sure whether I left of my own accord or whether I was eventually expelled for misbehavior."[26] Several years later Marquand accepted the commission to write a new novel about Moto for magazine publication. He explained to readers when it appeared that "I enjoy working on a somewhat abstract literary problem; I haven't done an adventure mystery in a long while; and this one would be interesting."[27]

Several points help account for the inconsistencies in the writer's views of his friends and their influence on his work. First might be cited his widely noticed lack of self-assurance and poise as a young man, something that undoubtedly made him susceptible to the will and advice of the older men who served as his mentors, and that in later years sometimes took the forms of heavy drinking and procrastination on difficult projects.[28] On many occasions his statements simply reflect the counselor or pressure prevailing at the time. Certainly the breakdown of his second marriage reduced Adelaide's influence and attempts to direct his career. A second observation is that Marquand and his principal magazine outlet came to symbolize the issues in a literary battle then being fought between America's intellectuals and its popular magazines. The former disdained the fame and money that accompanied success in the mass publications; the latter rejected the social criticism and artistic trends the intelligentsia considered valuable. To many intellectuals Marquand and the *Saturday Evening Post* represented the enemy: producers of escapist writing that might be technically good but was still not worth reading. In 1937 Marquand's role became more difficult as his pursuit of both levels of writing led him to be called a literary "split personality." Perhaps a third point is the author's obstinacy based on sincere love of both kinds of writing.[29] He might have fared better had he referred to his light fiction as either training exercises or simple entertainments. But instead he often felt compelled to defend all his works, insisting there were genuine skills that went into magazine writing, and claiming reviewers and critics were too biased to respect diversity.

The commissioning of all but one of the Moto stories by editors of the *Saturday Evening Post*[30] helped determine just how Marquand conceived his works and handled their content. Basic among the constraints was the need to produce a type of tale that possessed proven appeal, told a solid story in a straightforward and easily followed manner, involved people whose unusual lives and problems would engage readers' attention, and offended no one by very much deviation from the middle ground of its prospective audience's views. In this sense all the components—vocabulary, style, theme, structure, plot, length, characterization—had to conform to implicit rules. On the two occasions when Marquand attempted something different, in

1941 by testing Americans' anti-Japanese feelings with *Last Laugh, Mr. Moto,* and in 1956 by having heroine Ruth Bogart brutally killed in *Stopover: Tokyo,* he discovered that American magazine editors would resist publication. But even with creative freedom thus restricted, his pride in good craftsmanship continued to prevail and lent the stories merit despite their limitations.

An attempt to find the most apt term to describe the genre or subgenre of the Moto stories quickly reveals the unsuitability of many standard labels for identifying this particular series of works. Broad terms suffer from vagueness and subjective interpretation; narrow ones are too restrictive or even exclusive. The six novels themselves create the problem: individually, they are hybrid in nature; collectively, they form a disparate group. Simple labels—mysteries, thrillers, adventures—are inadequate. Although Marquand referred to the works as mysteries,[31] they lack the sustained mental challenge that word usually conveys, despite some occasional doubts about Moto's intentions. Several of the stories also have qualities associated with the thriller, such as shifting scenes and desperate races *(No Hero, Mr. Moto Is So Sorry)*, but others show little or no movement *(Thank You, Mr. Moto, Last Laugh, Mr. Moto)*. Probably more appropriate would be a category like "adventures," because it covers a wide range of content. All such labels need some complementary word, however, to identify the specific subgrouping in question. Many possibilities exist. The most fitting modifiers would be "spy" or "action" to indicate basic themes or approach. Yet the espionage motif is not always central *(Think Fast, Mr. Moto)*, and action sometimes is replaced by intrigue *(Thank You, Mr. Moto)*. On balance the safest and most readily defended subgenre is nevertheless that of the spy story. But however else individual titles may be described—action adventures, spy thrillers, tales of intrigue, romantic mysteries, escapist entertainments—they all formed part of a slowly emerging trend. One can hardly criticize an experimenting pioneer for not exhibiting the perfection or purity of form that specialists who came later have achieved. Marquand was too imaginative a writer to content himself with turning out a series of novels that followed a single pattern in describing the activities of Moto. Instead he valued the very changes that make classification of the series so difficult.

Although the Moto plots have been individually summarized, it is instructive to examine them as a group, for collectively they reveal much about Marquand's techniques. He could be inventive only within certain limits: for example, at the outset his editors had indicated they wanted settings in China, and his narrative style had to consider reader habits and tastes. His travels during 1934 and 1935 gave him enough notes and impressions to use backgrounds in China and Japan with relative ease. The amount of detail he incorporated—about the former capital in *Thank You, Mr. Moto* and the long rail journey in *Mr. Moto Is So Sorry*—depended upon his sureness of feeling. Admitting he could never know China well enough to write about it,[32] he rarely portrayed its people or problems except in the light of international rivalries, and yet the atmosphere of strife-torn China constitutes a compelling presence.[33] Although the author's sympathies obviously lay with the country in its plight, his stories could not offer solutions to its difficulties, except perhaps to raise his readers' awareness of such world events. Although the Moto novels are certainly not allegories, they might be seen in such a light as attempts to move Americans to greater involvement.[34] The writer himself was moving in that direction during the time he wrote the prewar stories. Thus the heroes who move from apathy or personal concerns to action and broader purpose might reasonably be seen also as the author's implicit recommendation to his readers. When the later tales moved away from Chinese settings they lost atmosphere and even interest. Neither of the last stories (*Last Laugh, Mr. Moto, Stopover: Tokyo*) has the earlier works' richness. Marquand had a personal and political feeling for China that he never possessed for the Caribbean or for aggressive and westernized Japan.

Two structural patterns appear in the six novels. Three stories are told as third-person narratives, moving through events in simple order; the other three use a personal recollection as the frame. Marquand also used the latter device in his major novels. This approach allows the reader to identify from the outset with the narrator during a critical or dangerous experience.[35] In his best fiction the crisis is most likely to be emotional or psychological; in the lighter works the ordeal is invariably physical but also marks a turning point. Thus even in the beginning of *No Hero* we know Casey Lee has survived a test that has reformed him; Tom Nelson immediately intrigues the reader by his opening observations on past events in *Thank You, Mr. Moto*; the voice in *Last Laugh, Mr. Moto* is third-person but the recollections begin even with the novel's opening sentence:

> When Robert Bolles tried to put all the events in order, his mind would keep going back to Mercator Island, although he knew that Mercator Island was nearer the end than the beginning.

The remainder of the paragraph then offers allusions to scenes and conflicts designed to tantalize the prospective reader. It is worth noting in particular that the heroes of all these novels would have little appeal if they were met initially as they had been when their stories began. When the author conceived more admirable or purposeful characters, as in the other novels, he felt no need to introduce them as already rehabilitated.

In other respects his plot structures are conventional. He positions a rather ordinary person in a situation in which he or she will be caught up in important events beyond his or her previous experience. Occasionally he glamorized the hero by making him someone rather unusual, like a flier, because the status added romantic images and explained any special skills. But nearly all the prewar spy novels adhered to the notion that espionage was an unsavory field, unsuitable for respectable people, who might nevertheless find themselves temporarily caught up in some extraordinary circumstances. They had to remain what readers expected of basically decent young men and women. Marquand's last two novels in the series could introduce professional agents as heroes only because of attitudinal changes created by patriotism in World War II.

Excitement in the plots results from both rapid pacing and mounting suspense. The least action-oriented of the stories is the rather moody *Thank You, Mr. Moto; Think Fast, Mr. Moto* attempts a similar aura of danger and mystery but ultimately fails. Its plot moves slowly enough to allow readers to question the thin premise on which it rests. Marquand liked to use a sustained search for some missing object or information in plotting the Motos. Certainly the approach is serviceable if not innovative in writing adventure tales. There were quests for a message and formula *(No Hero)*, rare paintings and plans *(Thank You, Mr. Moto)*, a secret involving money transfers *(Think Fast, Mr. Moto)*, a cigarette case and message *(Mr. Moto Is So Sorry)*, a valuable new aircraft device *(Last Laugh, Mr. Moto)*, and the identity of a top Communist agitator *(Stopover: Tokyo)*. Even in the non-series *Ming Yellow* he used the treasure motif. Not all such searches were central components of the stories, but they provided either an underlying motive or a continuing thread in the narratives, and hidden secrets are a mainstay of the spy story.

Treasure hunts to be interesting require relatively large numbers of diverse participants. The author usually assembled such an intriguing group, varied in nationality and background, each person pursuing some goal with intensity. From time to time the players form expedient alliances without ever losing sight of their ultimate aims. Such assemblies of mutually suspicious adventurers are occasionally highly effective *(Thank You, Mr. Moto, Mr. Moto Is So Sorry)* but sometimes fail to generate the chemistry the writer wanted *(Think Fast, Mr. Moto, Last Laugh, Mr. Moto).*[36] Marquand's biggest problem in the stories set in China was explaining the presence of the various Americans: the weakest reason is that provided for Calvin Gates in *Mr. Moto Is So Sorry,* but Tom Nelson's in *Thank You, Mr. Moto* may also strike readers as somewhat inadequate. The difficulty stems from Marquand's conception of his heroes.

The heroes of the Moto adventures are not unlike those in Marquand's major novels. A persistent theme in all his works involves the young man who has fallen from wealth or position, becoming déclassé or unwelcome in a world to which he seeks to belong, and who often blames his family for the financial ruin or lost opportunities that have blighted his life. Many of the author's writings offer mythic versions of his own youth, fictionalized to fit various plot situations, but revealing a father or authority figure as the cause of problems. The father-family theme appears in *Think Fast, Mr. Moto,* Eva Hitchings having been nearly destroyed by a black-sheep father and Wilson Hitchings having become narrow and dull under the influence of a staid family, and again in *Mr. Moto Is So Sorry,* where responsibility for a cousin's forgery has been chivalrously assumed by Calvin Gates. Examples of the authority-figure theme may be found in *No Hero, Thank You, Mr. Moto,* and *Last Laugh, Mr. Moto.* In *Thank You, Mr. Moto* Tom Nelson thinks he was unfairly treated by his law firm; the heroes of the other two novels are remarkably similar: both Casey Lee and Bob Bolles are former navy fliers who drink too much and blame the military service or their country for career disappointments. It is highly probable that Marquand identified with these troubled heroes, for such repetition in theme and portrayal matches what is known about his lifelong resentment of his father, and also because his adventure fiction let Marquand enjoy the excitement he craved. How family relationships and particular environments affect a young man is a theme that also permeates his serious fiction.[37] It is much better done there because the elaboration and subtlety of longer novels enabled him to achieve great effectiveness. But critics who disregard or dismiss his lighter fiction in their analyses of Marquand's writings miss an important linkage of theme and examples of its occurrence.

Rehabilitation became one of the principal necessities in characterization of the heroes. Nearly always achieved through unexpected involvement in critical events, combined with romantic interest in an attractive young woman, the transformations are often too abrupt to be realistic. When the stories are read as books, the rapidity with which the heroes change is more noticeable than when they are read as extended serials. As victims of what they consider to be parental or societal actions, the heroes begin as passive, demoralized, shallow, cynical, or selfish young men, people who must be brought back to productive life and self-esteem. The pattern appeared early and in its most extreme form with Casey Lee in *No Hero*; Tom Nelson in *Thank You, Mr. Moto* says repeatedly, "It doesn't matter, does it?"; Wilson Hitchings and Calvin Gates each must learn to look beyond narrow family or personal interests; Bob Bolles in *Last Laugh, Mr. Moto* has to overcome bitterness toward the United States Navy. In this respect as in others, *Stopover: Tokyo* is an exception among the Moto stories, for the characters are less formulaic. But all the prewar heroes must abandon their listlessness or inflexibility, discovering new purpose and values through proving themselves under challenge, their reward being greater self-knowledge and a girl's love, but the price being necessary compromise and recognition of past boorishness. Marquand did not always succeed in making his heroes convincing, especially with the motivation for Calvin Gates's long journey and sacrificing attitude, but he could sometimes be artfully subtle in characterization, as when he has the stuffy Wilson Hitchings not know what a sampan is, despite the fact that for six months he has lived in Shanghai. The revelation speaks eloquently of the man's isolation from his surroundings.

Each narrative includes a strain of romantic love, but it never dominates and seldom intrudes, remaining understated until the story reaches its end. Marquand had often been advised to expand the role of romance in his writings by the ever-market-conscious Brandt. That he minimized its presence in the Moto stories undoubtedly reflected both his discomfort with writing such scenes and his conviction that the Moto novels possessed a much more mixed appeal. There are certainly no scenes of strong passion or obvious sex in the stories. Yet in five narratives a blossoming love interest helps the hero find his way out of a life marked by indifference to his fate or even bitterness. Loss of a lover in the final novel has the opposite effect—the hero also loses his earlier strong sense of commitment and drive.

The author's ways of having his potential lovers meet and initially distrust each other followed well-established patterns of romantic fiction: his first two stories have the heroes find the women to whom they are attracted standing over corpses *(No Hero, Thank You, Mr. Moto)*; in others they are predetermined opponents *(Think Fast, Mr. Moto)* or suspect each other of disloyal associations *(Mr. Moto Is So Sorry)*; the heroines of two stories are professional agents who must work with the heroes on related or common aims *(Last Laugh, Mr. Moto, Stopover: Tokyo)*. All but the postwar novel follow the usual love-story development of attraction, conflict, and resolution or reconciliation after the various doubts and misunderstandings have been overcome. In the first four stories the heroes and heroines are set to marry as the adventure ends, in the fifth their future remains vaguely uncertain because of divergent commitments, and in the final story the woman's murder by enemy agents conveys the starker postwar realism. Both of these last heroines are trained operatives with their own objectives. Only in the postwar novel was there no difficulty between the lovers; the conflict there lay between emotions and the rules of their work. The magazine editors objected to that story's downbeat ending, however, believing the romantic element in light reading ought not be tragic. Yet only in that novel does the love interest achieve any deep impact on readers.

Very few of his female characters possess real dimension, but the vagueness of their backgrounds and attitudes makes them more believable than the heroes, for there is less reason to resist accepting them. They are attractive middle-class young women, apparently in their mid-twenties to thirty, pursuing careers or interests of their own, combining intelligence with common sense and spirit, and capable of decisive action when necessary. Each seems to represent the type of talented and successful woman the author admired—Carol Brandt, Helen Howe, Ray Murphy—rather than the decorative or socialite kind of woman he twice sought as wives. The occupations of his heroines were undoubtedly chosen carefully: they had to appeal to the romantic yearnings of the magazines' women readers, provide a plausible reason for travel to distant and dangerous places, and still be considered suitably feminine by the social codes of the period. Such a woman might assist a scientist father (Sonya Karaloff), buy art for a museum (Eleanor Joyce), run a family business (Eva Hitchings), be a professional artist (Sylvia Dillaway), or serve as an intelligence agent (Helen Kingman, Ruth Bogart). The last-named career is not as unusual as it may seem, for there is an established convention of the female agent or counterspy, and the author used them in wartime or cold war tales, when the impact of patriotism and service helped modify older societal notions. But the role of the female characters in the stories was consistently secondary, helping the troubled heroes when assistance was needed, but letting them prove their worth to themselves and others by acting alone.

One further point concerning characterization is worth noting. The author showed little imagination in naming his characters, using simple personal and family forms that would neither offend nor slow his readers, but his choices for foreign names were indeed odd. All the leading American male charcters had rather commonplace names—Casey Lee, Tom Nelson, Wilson Hitchings, Calvin Gates, Bob Bolles, Jack Rhyce—including the stuffy young banker; only the Russian woman's name broke the pattern among females—Sonya Karaloff, Eleanor Joyce, Eva Hitchings, Sylvia Dillaway, Helen Kingman, Ruth Bogart—because ethnic recognizability was needed. But occasional similarities in the sounds of names within a work may strike the reader as indicating limited ingenuity: for example, major characters named William, Wilson, and Wilkie in *Think Fast, Mr. Moto,* or the couple named Kingman appearing as Kingston in *Last Laugh, Mr. Moto.* More curious still is the likeness in forms chosen for various foreigners: Takahara and Ahara for the Japanese officials in *Thank You, Mr. Moto* and *Mr. Moto Is So Sorry,* Spirov and Skirov for the Russian agents in *Mr. Moto Is So Sorry* and *Stopover: Tokyo,* and Wu for the Chinese conspirator in *No Hero,* warlord in *Thank You, Mr. Moto,* and prince in *Mr. Moto Is So Sorry.* The existence of such patterns certainly adds weight to the evidence that the author worked hurriedly and reduced his stories to salable formulas. Marquand also ran into an unforeseen problem involving the name Moto. That situation is discussed later in this chapter in conjunction with the writer's conception of his title character.

Marquand's depictions of the world of international espionage were quite sophisticated by standards of the mid-1930s.[38] He applied all he had experienced and learned during his travels in Japan and China from both his own observations and stories told by newsmen. Those insights appeared throughout the series but are most pronounced in three of the novels: *No Hero, Last Laugh, Mr. Moto,* and *Stopover: Tokyo.* Marquand initially portrayed the competition of intelligence services as a special type of game, played by rules the professionals understood and generally honored, the agents respecting each other in ways exemplified by the behavior of Moto. But the outbreak of war hardened the author's approach into the realism so evident in his last two stories for the series. Surveying the writer's general comments on spying and agents is especially instructive as background for examining his handling of his famous character.

The distinction the author made between professional intelligence agents and the ordinary people caught up in some unusual situation allowed him to let the professionals occasionally explain the true nature of espionage work to the naïve outsiders. Although they described their world as one in which stark realism governed both objectives and relationships with other people, the effect conveyed to readers was still intended to be exciting and romantic, especially since the denouements of the stories left thwarted or dead only those hardened professionals who had been most unscrupulous or dangerous. For the others involved there was a happy or at least tolerable ending to the adventure. Each of the three novels in which the spy motif is most prominent may be used to illustrate aspects of the author's conception of the agents' world.

Soberness of tone in discussing espionage activities marked the very first story. An American intelligence officer and the beautiful Russian operative both caution the inexperienced American hero. Commander Driscoll tells Casey Lee, "There's no honor in this business. . . . We're dealing with realities and not with any code of chivalry. That belongs to another incarnation, but not in the Intelligence Service; that's a fact which is recognized by everyone in the game." He also expresses the professional's callousness when he asks the hero to obtain information from the woman: "A woman is always the weak link in such an affair as this. She can pry the secrets from the diplomat, and the gigolos can get the secrets from the ladies." But the intelligence officer respects his opponents:

> The people one encounters are much the same. They may be shady and raffish, but don't forget they're all of them brave. They do their work like pieces on a chess-board and nothing stops them from moving along their diagonals. You mustn't feel animosity toward them, Lee, for they feel none toward you. They're working for their respective countries and that's more than a lot of people do.

Sonya Karaloff's commitment to the White Russian cause had made her discourage Lee's romantic interest by saying, "No one should like anyone in this business," but of course Lee wins Sonya away from her espionage work at the conclusion of *No Hero*. By then he has come to realize that "international espionage moves in a world of its own" where neither personal feelings nor lives really matter.[39]

Special qualities attributed to experienced professional agents are brought out in *Last Laugh, Mr. Moto* to suggest still further how their work separates them from ordinary people. Agents must be single-minded and self-sacrificing in pursuit of their goals:

> They were there to do a piece of work, and nothing would stop them—no scruples, no thought of personal injury. They were carefully trained graduates of the most dangerous school in the world, so well-trained that they could keep their tempers and their wits, so well-trained that they could control every tremor of fear and nervousness.

But the agent's life often gave him or her a tell-tale look unlikely to escape notice by others in the field. Helen Kingman explains the point to Kingman and also refers to Moto:

> One can tell if one has been in the profession. Why, one can pick out the others like us in a crowded street. I saw it in your face even before I met you. Why, anyone can read it on this Japanese.
>
> It's the everlasting lying . . . the everlasting trying to laugh and to smile when you're afraid, the watching and the danger.

She adds that Bob Bolles lacks the look.[40] Agents also communicate in special ways: Moto knew by "a gesture and a glance" from Helen that she wanted him to kill Kingman. For those in the game there are both an absence of rancor and a certain mutual respect: they are opposing players who know that in the end some will win and others must lose. They accept either outcome philosophically if the match has been fair in the playing. Such professionalism and fatalism repeatedly induce the observing American heroes to look upon Moto and some of his rivals with near admiration. Marquand sensed throughout the series how important it was always to provide interesting counterparts and worthy opponents for the challenged but clever Moto.

All of the principal characters in *Stopover: Tokyo* are agents of competing governments. Although the novel offers the author's most complete treatment of the world of espionage, reflecting both his wartime experiences and the anti-Communist anxieties of the postwar period, its depiction of intelligence operations is built upon the earlier patterns and realism of the series. Learning once again of a grave danger posed by the Soviet Union, Moto schemes to uphold the interest of Japan, but America has now assumed a crucial role in events. Among new elements designed to intensify the novel's realism is the notion that even the hero-agents are fallible and make costly mistakes. Each of the main players has been careless: Ben Bushman gives away his identity by a fondness for tunes from *The Red Mill;* Jack Rhyce had once foolishly called attention to himself in Moscow, and his recognition now by a Soviet agent brings about the kidnapping and death of Ruth Bogart; Moto delays his quarry's capture when he misreads the evidence and falsely accuses Rhyce. But Marquand understood better than his magazine editors that he had to offer more than routine conflict and a happy ending in a spy story intended for 1950s readers. By making the female lead a professional agent, and then having her killed, he underscored the hard facts of espionage work: agents function in a field without scruples, pursue assignments without regard to personal feelings, accept risk to their lives without protest, and experience loneliness without open complaint. Marquand also used this final novel to reveal twenty years of reflection about the enigmatic Moto. His previous avoidance of detail concerning the character allowed him to fill in explanations with little difficulty over possible inconsistencies.

Marquand followed no preconceived scheme in developing the character of Moto. Instead the evidence makes clear that he worked his way into the series by circumstantial steps. The *Saturday Evening Post*'s offer to Marquand early in 1934 contained its editors' firm suggestions if not binding instructions: the magazine wanted stories set in contemporary Peking and northern China and featuring an attractive Chinese character. That Marquand understood his task is manifest from a February letter.[41] Yet it is not difficult to see why he chose to interpret the assignment loosely. Certainly he would seek to avoid merely varying the popular Chan figure, but he also realized that he could never know Chinese customs and outlooks well enough to portray a Chinese man living within his own culture and honoring its traditions. Marquand also felt uncomfortable about a continuing character and plot pattern. Thus it is significant that Moto did not appear until the author's second novel using China as a setting and that the magazine had to urge Marquand to produce sequels to it. Moreover, the use of a focal character who operated in a foreign environment and had to remain a man of mystery enabled the writer to omit troublesome details about cultural subtleties or personal history. He compensated for such superficiality by offering richness in travel information and atmosphere.

The inspiration for Moto seems reasonably clear. That Marquand developed his famous character by elaborating upon his own experience is borne out by statements he made in a 1957 interview. He spoke of Japanese treatment of Americans before the war: "I was constantly followed by Japanese detectives who used to search my baggage almost every night. They all of them looked and talked exactly like Mr. Moto."[42] Such Japanese security men thus served as the model for the Moto character. But even though Marquand gave his fictional creation a certain degree of wit and charm, enough to make him acceptable or even likable to readers, the author himself never overcame his early antipathy to the nation Moto served. Not only had he not liked the country on his first visit, objecting to both cultural changes and obsessive suspicion, but he also became even more critical in later years over its aggressions. As early as summer 1939 he referred to Japan as "an arrogant nation" that understood only force. By then it was becoming clear that the more belligerent elements among the country's leaders were gaining control. His reaction to Pearl Harbor was especially strong. Combined with his lifelong hatred of the Germans, stemming from his World War I experiences and even in the mid-1950s still quite evident, such feelings made him deeply oppose the Axis.[43] That attitude is clear in *Last Laugh, Mr. Moto,* in which all enemies are defeated. His views were scarcely modified in the postwar years, even though he made Japan the scene of the last adventure, for he pointedly revealed Moto's strong sense of national pride, showing there were still undercurrents of dangerous nationalism. And he allowed the only racial slur in the series to appear in the postwar adventure: Jack Rhyce in anger calls Moto a "little yellow bastard." It is helpful to bear in mind the author's mixed feelings about his character and the nation he represented as a profile of the agent is drawn from the six novels of the series.

Physical descriptions of Moto remained minimal because Marquand considered them unnecessary. Clearly the character was intended to be both typical of his countrymen and yet somewhat memorable as an individual. The effect of Moto's overall appearance was summarized in the last novel by the American intelligence agent: "Once more Jack Rhyce had the impression of a character that was too Japanese to be true."[44] But closer scrutiny of the novels reveals a number of qualities out of the ordinary.

Details about specific features are scattered throughout the stories. Casey Lee offered the first description of him in *No Hero:* "He was small, almost delicate . . . little feet, little hands." Later he is called "a small man, delicate, almost fragile," who walked with "swift birdlike steps," had a "row of shiny gold-filled teeth," and brushed his black hair "in the Prussian style." We are also told that the effect of "his round head and his black hair arranged in a shoebrush pattern was almost grotesque" when he put on western evening clothes. The last prewar novel adds the detail that he had "high cheekbones, narrow jaw and narrow dark eyes," but he is never described as wearing glasses, so prominent in his appearance as seen by millions of filmgoers. In middle age he remained unchanged except that his hair was "grayish," but still "close-cropped," so that he preserved the special air of a former military man.[45]

Moto's choice of clothes was a source of running humor, the only real such element in the novels, for he liked to copy the dress of stylish westerners. Yet the results were never quite right despite his claim of having served as a valet. The absence of a good sense of occasion and appropriateness, plus an apparent problem with color, gave his appearance all sorts of odd and incongruous effects. Marquand undoubtedly introduced this comic touch to suggest the cultural changes he had observed taking place in prewar Japan. Moto often appeared in formal dress—dinner jacket and pleated shirt, double-breasted evening wear "cut in extreme lines," morning coat with striped trousers—wearing patent-leather shoes that squeaked. On other occasions he might wear "a tweed golf suit and a brown tweed cap," something in loud checks, or "a business suit of an unpleasant purplish blue color" with "very yellow tan shoes,"[46] thinking such outfits suitable. The author liked his character too much to dwell on such matters in a way that might make him seem ridiculous. But he could not resist recurring wry comments on the pitfalls of incomplete absorption of another culture.

Only one other physical quality of Moto was noted repeatedly in the stories. For reasons attributable to either his cultural mannerisms or his dental work, Moto produced a sound that other characters described as "sibilant," for he "breathed with a peculiar little hiss,"[47] and spoke the same way. The effect was not displeasing, however, and complemented his customary politeness. Marquand had undoubtedly observed the tendency to sibilancy among the Japanese. Adding such detail to the portrayal of Moto helped to make him seem more authentic.

Marquand maintained an aura of mystery around his character by refusing to give any but fragmentary facts about Moto. Although the initial omission of detail probably stemmed from space limitations in the magazine serial format, especially when the character was neither central to the narrative nor expected to reappear in subsequent stories, the author recognized the advantages in continuing to keep his hero's background a source of conjecture. There are only occasional references to Moto's past life and his professional experiences. One might be tempted to dismiss even those hints as part of an agent's deliberate obfuscation of his real identity if the remarks did not come from the polite and sincere character in moments of relative ease.

Among the details the careful reader learns about Moto are his upper-class lineage and extensive travels. In the very first novel the American hero describes him as a "most accomplished gentleman" and "suave scion of the Japanese nobility" whom he found likable. The third story gives readers more clues about him. Moto says he has been to "very many places in both Europe and America during the course of my work and my education," "was in the Navy once," and has "served whiskey so often to gentlemen in America" when he was employed there as a valet. His education had included studies in an American university. He had also been in Berlin and Vladivostok on assignments for his country. But the final story, *Stopover: Tokyo,* offers the fullest details. Moto reveals that his father was in the Japanese consulate in New York in 1912 and that a big house in Japan belongs to a baron who is his cousin; the house has been in Moto's family for centuries. He confides that "before everything was so unhappy, I was over once a year at least, New York, Washington, or Honolulu. Even when my duties were in Paris and London I endeavored to spend a week or two of observation in New York."[48]

Moto nevertheless apologetically understated his excellent command of English. Even in the first novel an American considered it very good, and he had no trouble with the English *l* unless some role called for the pretense, but the war years of the 1940s had caused rustiness. He also confessed in the 1950s that newer American idioms and slang troubled him. Yet it may strike readers throughout the series as rather odd that Moto copes easily with unusual words and constructions but hesitates with simpler terms. We might also infer from his travels and European assignments that he knew French and perhaps other languages at least reasonably well. And Moto confided without boasting that he knew five Chinese dialects.[49]

His breadth of experience had also given Moto many practical skills and great resourcefulness. He modestly confessed, "Yes, I can do many, many things" because "so very many things come in useful."[50] His naval training undoubtedly explains his demonstrated knowledge of navigation, the handling of boats, and the repair of a diesel engine on a disabled cabin cruiser. On other occasions he admitted to being a "very good valet," someone who "can mix drinks and wait on table," and a craftsman skilled in the arts of "carpentry and surveying." And of course he handled arms and various means of self-defense with the ease that comes with training and use.

In many ways Moto's westernization remained a veneer for the benefit of Americans and others. Often he appears merely to emulate the life of gentlemen he had known or observed: on several occasions he drinks whiskey and soda in moderation when the indulgence seems companionable, he plays bridge, and he smokes cigarettes even while admitting they leave traces and smells that betray an agent. Yet his westernization did not extend to inner values and concepts—either in matters of national pride or in notions of beauty. Proud of Japan's culture and able to speak with ease of its art, he admits he could never fully understand Western art, though he had been to "so many of your great galleries in Europe."[51] In another conversation he confided that European women were not beautiful to him. But he accepted their personal freedom and abilities, complimented them on their appearance, and treated them with great tact and courtesy. At least two women had nevertheless tricked him in ways he always remembered as professional embarrassments.

Marquand emphasized in his character the extreme politeness of the Japanese. Sometimes the agent's courtesy was overdone to further his aims, creating an ingratiating or obsequious manner when it was useful, and his habit of overapologizing could often be annoying. Casey Lee observed in No Hero, "He kept saying he was so very, very sorry," and Marquand entitled one tale Mr. Moto Is So Sorry. But his consideration toward those he liked or respected was genuine and repeatedly demonstrated. Sonya assured Lee in No Hero that Moto was not a villain but "a very considerate man."[52] The instances where he showed deep sensitivity and understanding toward others underscore the point. When Bushman is finally caught and must be killed in Stopover: Tokyo, Moto takes responsibility for the prisoner from Rhyce, saying the American should not have to carry Bushman's death on his conscience. A similar intervention in Thank You, Mr. Moto had helped its protagonist.

Marquand's polite agent became a personification of modern Japan. Moto combined qualities associated with the old society and values—intelligence, cleverness, determination, subtlety, resourcefulness, modesty, courtesy—with mastery of the technology and methods of the West. But the formal rituals and underlying values of the West baffled or eluded him. The author at first showed the gap in such obvious matters as inappropriate use of western clothes; in the last two novels he was more explicit in detailing his character's unchanged beliefs and attitudes. To see Moto most accurately we must examine what Marquand wrote of him as a lifelong Japanese agent. There we see more of the substance the writer saw beneath the surface politeness.

Moto revealed in the series' first novel that he entered his country's intelligence service in the late 1920s. He would probably then have been in his mid-twenties since he was described as about fifty a decade after the war. But this chronology also means that he was only thirty or so at the time of the first story—certainly a rather young age for an operative to have the degree of authority he so clearly exercised. He was proud of the old service, confiding that "we had such a very lovely Intelligence system before the war," for then "the machinery was not bad." But postwar operations suffered from lack of funds and "poor Japan" had fallen behind other nations in the intelligence field.[53] The nationalist feelings evident in such expressions of nostalgia and regret are not unexpected given the character's earlier attitudes.

In keeping with his class and military background, Moto believed strongly in what he envisioned as a special destiny for Japan, although he seemed reasonable compared with others. That he separated himself from the extremists, and repeatedly opposed fanatics within his country's army, does not diminish his own chauvinism. Marquand made his character's expansionist position apparent all through the series but seldom allowed anything concrete to be said about Moto. It is interesting that the two most revealing statements about his views may be found in the first and last stories—in one instance before any thought that there might be a series and in the other when the author no longer cared. Such frankness during the course of the series' run would have been awkward.

Casey Lee observed in *No Hero* that Moto wanted Japanese-American friendship "as long as that amity did not interfere with what he and his own political faction conceive to be his nation's divine mission to establish a hegemony in the East."[54] Marquand made the Soviet Union the principal enemy of such an empire and reasoned that his readers would object to the Communist Soviet Union more than Japan. But in the first four novels the real victim of Japanese aggression was shown to be a weak and helpless China caught between the ambitions of its two more powerful neighbors. Moto often opposed the methods of some of his countrymen, because they were risky or unnecessary, but never the right of his nation to dominate China. By *Stopover: Tokyo* Moto identified himself as a member of the postwar Nationalist Japan Party and described it as representing the old Japan, "Fascist, perhaps, but pro-Emperor, anti-Communist."[55] Thus he remained a committed nationalist who implied that defeated Japan's cooperation with the Americans was acceptable because prevailing conditions seemed to permit no alternative. The Moto of the books was clearly not the benign neutral of the Hollywood films.

Throughout the series Marquand showed that Moto could be ruthless. As courteous as he might appear under ordinary circumstances, Moto never forgot that he served Japan, reluctantly accepting the fact that his duties might involve brutality. In *No Hero* when he told an uncooperative Casey Lee that he would have his men interrogate the hero, Moto confessed that "I dislike certain parts of my profession very much," and later Sonya also assured Lee that Moto would kill him if he still refused to surrender the message. When Lee referred to that as murder, Sonya observed, "I should rather call it a secret agent's life. If you had lived in my country you would know. It's part of the profession. You must not blame them. Don't you see, it's the only thing they can do?" In *Think Fast, Mr. Moto,* after an opponent's arm had been broken in a fight and pressure was placed on the injured arm because the man would not reveal key information, Moto told the American, "I do not like putting subjects to the question. It is a method with which I know you do not sympathize but in this case it is important." Nor in *Last Laugh, Mr. Moto,* in pursuing his own goals, would he have interfered to stop Kingman from killing Bolles. Moto was also prepared to torture Jack Rhyce in *Stopover: Tokyo* when he thought Rhyce worked for the Soviet Union. Moto told the intended victim that "Moscow does not know all the tricks." Yet in none of the stories did he ever harm an American hero, despite various threats. Nor would Moto resort to what he knew Americans called "a cheap trick" to gain some advantage because he proclaimed that "I am not cheap" or unprofessional.[56] Villains were nevertheless readily dispatched: he himself killed Takahara and Wu in *Thank You, Mr. Moto*

79

and Kingman in *Last Laugh, Mr. Moto*. Moto ordered the execution of Hamby in *Mr. Moto Is So Sorry*. But the most striking case occurs in *Stopover: Tokyo* when three enemy agents meet violent deaths: Bushman is led away for special interrogation and handling by the Japanese, Skirov falls from the eighth floor of a building in Tokyo, and Pender is reportedly killed by a truck after being caught by Moto.

During his long years of intelligence assignments Moto had become fatalistic about his own survival. In an early adventure he explained how extreme suspicion and caution had saved his life on several occasions, but he added, "So many people have tried to kill me. Please, we must all die sometime." Death did not frighten him as long as he had served his nation well. "So many things I do are dangerous. Besides, if I found out what I wish, I should be very, very pleased to die. If I do not find out, I am afraid that I must kill myself, so that all is very much the same." Moto confided similarly to another American, "My friend, I have had so many firearms pointed at me before that a man in my position is used to them. A servant of the emperor is not afraid of death. It is a glory to him when he serves his emperor."[57] And he is indeed prepared for suicide at the end of *Mr. Moto Is So Sorry* when he gambles with Spirov on what Moscow will do about Japan's military advances in northern China. Marquand never overdid the familiar "honor or death" attitude in characterization of Moto. But he had achieved such success early in the series that readers knew no real harm would come to the agent despite the many tight situations and the repeated assurances that he would accept death with calm resignation.

Marquand's sense of realism and drama accounts for his showing the human fallibility of Moto. Some revelations of past mistakes helped add dimension to the characterization; other errors involving misjudgments or miscalculations became devices to enhance suspense. Two examples of the former concern mistakes he made as a young agent who was rather gullible when it came to attractive women. He confessed that once in Washington "a lovely girl" had sold him "the Navy plans of a submarine" for thirty thousand yen, but the papers turned out to be blueprints for a tugboat, a deception that an ex–Imperial Navy man like Moto ought to have avoided without much difficulty. And in Tokyo a woman had lured Moto to a meeting in her garden, where her accomplices then tried to kill him, causing Moto to admit, "I do not understand lovely ladies, but still I trust them sometimes."[58] There are various instances of his errors in the novels' main adventures. Three examples from *Stopover: Tokyo* will suffice. In his guise as an anxious tourist guide for the visiting Americans he arouses their suspicion because he never tries to explain sights. When asked to order tea, Moto inadvertently asks for coffee in Japanese, and his error is overheard. It too raises questions about him. But the most important mistake is his ready assumption that Rhyce is "Big Ben" despite the flimsy evidence and his years of experience. Yet the stories benefit greatly from their readers' knowledge that Moto is neither superhuman nor always successful in his espionage work.

An especially interesting dimension of Moto's intelligence career is always understated. Bits of information clearly confirm that Moto operated in many countries, but readers might well overlook what was thus implied: there existed a Japanese spy system even in their own country. Moto's frequent visits to New York and other places could hardly have been made just to permit him to update his knowledge of American slang and colloquial English. That he did operate as an agent in American territory was made evident in *Think Fast, Mr. Moto* because he knew Hawaii and worked through local contacts in the islands. Moto also revealed in *Mr. Moto Is So Sorry* that he had been tricked in Washington over the American submarine plans; in *Last Laugh, Mr. Moto* he admitted trying to steal the secret aircraft device at the production plant in the United States. In *Stopover: Tokyo* he confided to Jack Rhyce that the American's prewar Japanese instructor in Colorado had worked under Moto's supervision. And the young Japanese man who approached Rhyce and Ruth Bogart in San Francisco was working for Moto after the war. Those who read the stories as thrillers probably did not pay much attention to such revelations or implications concerning the other activities of the high-ranking agent. Certainly his popularity with Americans depended to a great degree on his appearance as a qualified friend of their country and not as a Japanese spy working against them. But the unsympathetic Marquand repeatedly suggested what he believed was the true extent of Japan's worldwide espionage network.

For all of Moto's espionage activity before and after the war, he had nevertheless escaped the official notice of the major Washington analysts. In *Stopover: Tokyo* Marquand did not specifically refer to the Central Intelligence Agency, choosing to identify the "Chief" only by certain implications, but Jack Rhyce and Ruth Bogart are clearly sent to Japan by the CIA. Yet the "Chief" has never heard of Moto even though he had been a specialist on the Far East in the pre–World War II period. But *No Hero*'s Casey Lee had submitted a full report on the Japanese agent's activities during those years to American Naval Intelligence. Had Bob Bolles and the *Smedley*'s commander failed to report the events of *Last Laugh, Mr. Moto* in 1941? The point concerning Moto's obscurity is interesting. Marquand's consistency in handling information throughout the series makes mere oversight unlikely, but he might well have been trying to preserve his character's aura of mystery, or he may have been acknowledging the strong interagency rivalries in Washington. His own wartime work would have suggested that possibility as an explanation. But it seems odd that an operative and official as important as Moto had never acquired a thick dossier in the nation's top intelligence agency.

Marquand's carefulness avoided inconsistencies in characterization of his fictional agent, but he made one notable error: the designation of the operative by the improbable name I. A. Moto. After the choice apparently prompted some readers over the years to raise questions concerning its plausibility, Marquand himself introduced the topic in his postwar novel featuring Moto, thereby acknowledging in print that he had been made aware of the mistake that had occurred. There is no indication in the prewar stories that he sensed any problem, however, and also none that he had intended using an unlikely cover name. He just erred in assuming that the simple name would serve his need. Although the name is sometimes used as an abbreviated form of a given name, as, for example, Motokichi or Motojito, *Moto* cannot stand alone as a family name in Japan. It often appears as a suffix or final element in proper names, as in Yamamoto or Mikimoto. Its presence in such forms reflects its several meanings that vary according to context and combination: it may in one form mean a book, in others refer to a founder, to old times, or to a deceased person, or it may suggest a close tie.[59] Marquand was probably attracted to the name because it was short, easily remembered, and seemed to have a ring of authenticity to average Americans. The "I. A." initials were never explained in Marquand's stories.[60]

What makes the author's error important is the effect the name's impossibility has in undermining certain incidents in his narratives. Westerners might not become immediately suspicious upon hearing it, but Marquand's other Japanese characters and well-informed foreigners would quickly recognize its falseness. Therefore the agent's unobtrusive manner and behavior, so typical of his mode of working and so essential to many occasions, could hardly have been successful as described. Marquand tried to cover the error in *Stopover: Tokyo* by having Jack Rhyce become doubtful upon hearing the name Moto: he thinks he would have "bet his last dollar" that Moto was an intelligence agent "except for the clumsy use of a name that . . . was not a name at all."[61] No government operative would be expected to call attention to himself by using a patently false name.

A further point concerning the name suggests the broad popularity of the character: the designation "Mr. Moto" became "a generic term for Japanese early in the war" among American military personnel. Marquand acknowledged his awareness of such slang in a letter apparently written about 1945:

> In the first year of the Japanese war, I was much surprised to observe that the Japanese were frequently referred to as Mr. Moto by members of the Army, Navy, and Marines, and the term was occasionally used in the institutional advertizing [sic] of the period. Later in the war, however, Mr. Moto seemed to be entirely dropped and I don't believe it has any place in present military vernacular.[62]

Marquand ought not to have been surprised, given Americans' familiarity with his Moto character, probably the best known of all Japanese. But Moto had also become too attractive, especially in film treatments, to remain an object of American wrath. In that respect the name "Tojo" served to much better effect.

Evaluating the comparative merits of the six Moto novels requires that their differences be recognized. Dissimilarities in the natures of some of the stories make comparisons somewhat unfair or subject to qualifications. Certainly the postwar *Stopover: Tokyo* is most outstanding. Written after Marquand had published more than half a dozen major novels, it rises above its genre in many ways, but especially in its stark realism and fuller development of Moto's character. The plot is both solidly constructed and compelling, characterizations have subtlety, and the tone catches the somber postwar mood. It would be surprising if we did not find such attributes in a late work by a highly experienced novelist. Yet critical comparison of *Stopover: Tokyo* with the earlier popular adventures is justified perhaps only by Moto's presence in all of them.

Among the prewar stories the two weakest are most readily identified. In both cases Marquand used settings—Hawaii and the Caribbean—that lack China's color and mystery. Nor does either new background contribute much toward explaining the adventure as an integral part of its particular milieu. Thus the shifts of scene detract from the works' appeal without offering any compensating interest or purpose. Their other weaknesses, however, are quite dissimilar. *Think Fast, Mr. Moto* suffers from a flimsy plot line that must strike any but the most superficial reader as implausible; the plot is much sounder but the title character more stereotyped and less attractive and resourceful in *Last Laugh, Mr. Moto.* Although the latter novel is not the "perfunctory work" its creator thought, it does fall below the standard set in its predecessors, the result of Marquand's lack of genuine interest in the entire project.[63] Of the other three prewar stories, *No Hero* has fast pacing but little subtlety. Its strengths are those of all thrillers in which action substitutes for nuances of plotting and characterization.

Whether the best of the prewar novels is considered to be *Thank You, Mr. Moto* or *Mr. Moto Is So Sorry* depends on what a particular reader or analyst has in mind. *Thank You, Mr. Moto* stresses elements of mood, intrigue, character, and local setting, qualities more typical of the novel than of the adventure tale; by contrast, a journey, rivalries, danger, and excitement dominate *Mr. Moto Is So Sorry.* Both works hold up surprisingly well. But *Thank You, Mr. Moto* seems to merit the top ranking among the early Mr. Moto stories.[64] It possesses the important attributes of the other adventures as well as literary qualities not found in them or the genre in general.

NOTES

1. Marquand described the method in 1956: "The presence of the young lady, whom I am paying, stimulates me to be industrious, and a first draft, rapidly achieved before the later cutting, enables me to see more of the forest and become less entangled in the trees." *Saturday Evening Post,* 17 November 1956, p. 152. He was talking about *Stopover: Tokyo* and tactfully omitted the fact that Carol Brandt had typed the draft.

2. In putting together a collection of his short writings, *Thirty Years,* the author admitted he had overused some settings. See his foreword and also Birmingham, p. 257.

3. The agency was originally Brandt and Kirkpatrick but later became Brandt and Brandt when Carl's brother Erdman became a partner. Bell, pp. 119, 187.

4. Ibid., pp. 120–21, 275; Birmingham, pp. 45–46, 49–50, 65–66, 301–10.

5. Bell, pp. 229, 273–74, 276–77.

6. Ibid., p. 153.

7. The idea that Marquand wrote popular fiction only to support his more serious work received public exposure in 1938 through a friend. Constance Fiske wrote a profile published in the *Saturday Review of Literature*, 10 December 1938, p. 10, in which she suggested just that false explanation. Brandt saw it before publication and tried to prevent its appearance; he probably suspected the rationale stemmed from the notions of Adelaide. See Bell, pp. 258–59; Birmingham, pp. 119–21. Holman, p. 18, repeats the point asserted by Fiske.

8. George Horace Lorimer was editor of the *Saturday Evening Post* and also chairman of Curtis Publishing Company.

9. Bell, pp. 120–21, 259; Birmingham, pp. 45, 67. Marquand's lifetime income from the *Saturday Evening Post* came to more than $500,000. Birmingham, pp. 301–10, has a solid list of his various publications arranged by year.

10. Bell, p. 229.

11. Ibid., p. 249, quoting a letter from Brandt to Marquand, 29 November 1935.

12. McIntyre was at Little, Brown and Company when the author moved to it from Charles Scribner's Sons in 1929. The latter firm had published his first novels. But in 1929 Little, Brown and Company offered a very generous $1,000 advance for book rights to Marquand's serial called *Warning Hill*. The author's biographers concur that he switched publishers solely for the money involved. Birmingham, p. 50; Bell, p. 158. Marquand thus began a lifelong association with the company McIntyre later came to head before his death in 1948.

13. The publisher's reasons were both financial and artistic. It should be remembered that Brandt sent Marquand's novels to McIntyre and magazine editors simultaneously. Serialization gave the author public exposure but always cut potential book sales. Yet the publisher also felt that Marquand's magazine fiction was not his best.

14. Bell, pp. 256, 274.

15. Birmingham, p. 153.

16. See chapter 1, note 17.

17. Bell, p. 572.

18. Ibid., p. 574. In the early 1950s Marquand observed, "I was caught early in the meshes of what is unkindly but accurately called 'commercial writing'—a hard school and one which finally demands a broad knowledge of techniques" (Foreword, *Thirty Years*, p. xiv).

19. See Holman, p. 6.

20. "Why Did Mr. Moto Disappear?", *Newsweek*, 21 January 1957, p. 106.

21. Letter from Marquand to Brandt, 3 April 1939, quoted in Bell, p. 123.

22. Ibid., quoting a letter from Marquand to Marjorie Stoneman Douglas, 10 April 1939.

23. Ibid., quoting a letter from Marquand to Sergeant Jack Briggs, 16 April 1945.

24. Ibid., p. 403.

25. Ibid., p. 350. After 1940 Marquand did no more commissioned work for magazines and comparatively little light fiction at all until the 1950s Moto story. Ibid., p. 259.

26. Foreword, *Thirty Years*, pp. xiv–xvi. He argued that even the *New Yorker* and avant-garde publications have "equally dogmatic fashions" with regard to fiction: "The final result of these conventions, whether they are vulgar or artistic, is formula."

27. *Saturday Evening Post*, 24 November 1956, p. 152.

28. Helen Howe spoke of his "true inner lack of self-confidence" during the early 1930s. He was also socially inept until he gained experience. See Birmingham, pp. 33, 145.

29. Marquand always admired the finely wrought works of Jane Austen and Edith Wharton and considered the greatest novel to be *Madame Bovary*. Ibid., pp. 77, 173. His love of adventure stories has been explained. He was especially annoyed when critics subjected his lighter works to close scrutiny. Reacting to their remarks about the satirical *Life at Happy Knoll*, he complained, "It is fun and games, the book was written as fun and games! Can't they understand that?" Ibid., p. 283.

30. Only *Last Laugh, Mr. Moto* was written without a prior commitment from *Saturday Evening Post* editors. They rejected the manuscript when it was offered.

31. "Why Did Mr. Moto Disappear?", p. 106. He also called them "adventure mysteries" in the *Saturday Evening Post*, 24 November 1956, p. 152.

32. A restatement of the author's feelings of inadequacy occurs in *Melville Goodwin, U.S.A.* when the novel's narrator, Sidney Skelton, says he left Shanghai with "enthusiasms and illusions" but knew he lacked the ability ever to write about China. See Bell, p. 338.

33. In Bell's opinion the novelist's deft handling of the Chinese atmosphere deserved better story material than the Moto tales.

34. Bell, p. 221.

35. Holman points out that seven of Marquand's nine novels of manners do not have conventional plots. Instead he offered a man facing the crisis of his life and used memories to show how he reached that point. See p. 29.

36. One of the least effective characterizations is that of the gangster Paul Maddock in *Think Fast, Mr. Moto*. Marquand never succeeded in making him seem truly sinister, although he was clearly fashioned in the old Hollywood mold, repeatedly saying, "Snow, if you don't get my drift," to convey a menacing toughness. The failure of this character to seem genuinely ruthless undermines the dangerous interplay of various people and factions on which the plot rests. The ensemble of high-stakes players never seems to consist of real people.

37. On this general point see in particular Bell, pp. xiii, 220; Holman, p. 29; Birmingham, p. 28.

38. Before the mid-1930s the most common settings for spy tales were great country houses, embassies, and luxury hotels patronized by the rich and glamorous members of Europe's international set. The enormous output and success of snobbish E. Phillips Oppenheim (1866–1946) attest to readers' tastes

in the period. Qualities of romantic adventure were generally more important than disturbing elements of realistic depiction. Eric Ambler is credited with introducing far more realism in his spy novels of the second half of the 1930s.

39. The five quotations in this paragraph may be found in *No Hero* on pp. 175–76, 174, 6, 109, and 6, respectively.

40. The three long quotations appear in *Last Laugh, Mr. Moto* on pp. 144, 155, and 155–56.

41. Letter to Helen Howe, 11 February 1934, quoted in Bell, pp. 204–5. He told her the magazine wanted "a new Chinese character and a Chinese background" for the stories.

42. "Why Did Mr. Moto Disappear?", p. 106.

43. Letter from Marquand to Lester Walker, editor of *Commentator*, 26 July 1939, quoted in Bell, pp. 291–92. See also pp. 218, 298, 303.

44. *Stopover: Tokyo*, p. 169.

45. See *No Hero*, p. 168; *Think Fast, Mr. Moto*, pp. 155, 197; *Last Laugh, Mr. Moto*, p. 144; *Stopover: Tokyo*, p. 70.

46. See *No Hero*, pp. 89, 168–69, 237, 275; *Think Fast, Mr. Moto*, pp. 155, 197; *Stopover: Tokyo*, p. 70.

47. *No Hero*, p. 23. See also *Think Fast, Mr. Moto*, pp. 155, 215, and *Stopover: Tokyo*, pp. 105–6. It should be noted that Birmingham's description of Moto as "lisping" is not accurate. Nor is his use of "foot-shuffling" to describe the character. Birmingham, pp. 67, 78. Those qualities suggest the film portrayal rather than the novels' descriptions.

48. See *No Hero*, pp. 5–6; *Think Fast, Mr. Moto*, pp. 216, 226, 257, 269; *Last Laugh, Mr. Moto*, p. 153; *Stopover: Tokyo*, pp. 220, 223, 227.

49. *No Hero*, p. 168; *Think Fast, Mr. Moto*, p. 269; *Stopover: Tokyo*, p. 220.

50. *Think Fast, Mr. Moto*, pp. 257, 269.

51. Ibid., pp. 216, 226, 266–77; *Stopover: Tokyo*, p. 225.

52. *No Hero*, pp. 168–69, 236. Moto was even said to breathe "politely." *Think Fast, Mr. Moto*, p. 215.

53. *Stopover: Tokyo*, pp. 145, 220, 224, 225.

54. *No Hero*, p. 6. See also *Mr. Moto Is So Sorry*, pp. 257–58.

55. *Stopover: Tokyo*, pp. 227–28.

56. See *No Hero*, pp. 120, 126; *Think Fast, Mr. Moto*, p. 260; *Stopover: Tokyo*, pp. 213, 222–23; *Think Fast, Mr. Moto*, p. 226, respectively, for the information presented.

57. See *Think Fast, Mr. Moto*, pp. 215, 222; *Mr. Moto Is So Sorry*, p. 59.

58. *Mr. Moto Is So Sorry*, p. 252.

59. I appreciate greatly the help of Professor Tetsumaro Hayashi of Ball State University on Japanese meanings and uses of the name. He clarified the ways in which *moto* may and may not appear in Japanese in both personal and family names.

60. In the film *Mr. Moto's Last Warning*, Moto displayed the given name "Kenaro" on a sign. It obviously does not match the initials identified in the novels.

61. *Stopover: Tokyo,* pp. 100, 306. The hero also wondered if the distinctive clothes worn by Moto were not just a further clumsy attempt at fooling people. See pp. 105–6.

62. William White, "Mr. Marquand's 'Mr. Moto,'" *American Speech* 23 (April 1948), 157–58. White had investigated wartime use of the name and had written about it to Marquand.

63. Marquand's biographers disagree about *Last Laugh, Mr. Moto.* Bell, p. 219, calls it the "least effective" work in the series, but Birmingham, p. 154, considers it "a highly competent thriller" that keeps readers guessing. Holman, pp. 21–22, tends to agree with Bell.

64. Bell, p. 217, also accords first rank to *Thank You, Mr. Moto.*

IV

Moto in Hollywood

MR. MOTO'S POPULARITY with readers quickly led to interest on the part of Hollywood and prompted Twentieth Century–Fox to make eight Moto films from 1937 to 1939. Marquand had been only too glad to earn additional money by selling screen rights to his character and stories without being much concerned about how the filmmakers dealt with Moto. What they did was strange. A compelling reason for comparing the film treatments with the written stories is that the former had almost nothing to do with the latter. Yet those who know only the film productions, including a number of writers specializing in cinema studies, often attribute their plots to the published works. The error is perhaps understandable in the two instances where the original story titles were retained for the film productions. But it has led to numerous misconceptions about the stories and misstatements about the films that represent a disservice to the creations in each medium. Four aspects of the films warrant discussion to help correct the situation.

Hollywood studios found themselves facing a shortage of good material for film scripts during the mid-1930s. Especially in demand were stories that would make suitable popular entertainment, simple narratives that might be put on film cheaply but that would still draw sizable audiences, usually as part of a double-feature billing in neighborhood cinemas. Serial stories with recurring characters held particular interest for producers because successive film releases carried ready-made box-office recognition and appeal.[1] Marquand's adventures seemed to offer just what studios wanted, and film rights to the story material were easily sold starting in 1935. From the outset the studio planned a series—and at least initially one with solid merit. Moto films nevertheless quickly declined in both creative commitment and production quality until they became the type of highly formulized offering so attractive to the studios for financial reasons and so popular with bargain-hunting filmgoers in the 1930s. By then the Moto films had become just another B-level series. They might not even command top position in double billings, and they scarcely justified being reviewed upon their release. Exhaustion of the character and story possibilities, combined with production problems and changing market conditions, ended the series after just two years. Moto disappeared from the screen for twenty-six years after 1939.

Twentieth Century–Fox was a relatively new corporation when it acquired the film rights to Marquand's stories and was already the producer of the highly popular films featuring Charlie Chan.[2] Apparently studio executives thought there was room for a second such mystery series because they almost immediately transformed their acquisition into another detective.[3] Moto became merely a variation of Chan.[4] Perhaps it is understandable that the studio was wary of dealing with contemporary international intrigue, especially featuring a Japanese intelligence agent, but the change robbed the character of his substance and disregarded the original story lines. Also soon abandoned were the Oriental locales that had made the published tales and some early Moto films so colorful and unusual. In time the films caused those unacquainted with the printed stories to assume that their central figure had always been a detective.[5] Having decided to strip Moto of his profession, the task then confronting studio planners was how to make him and his films seem different from their other established series, a problem the Moto films never fully overcame.

Comparison of Moto and Chan is inevitable. They and their films had much in common, of course, but the differences between them were also important.[6] A brief survey of certain similarities is useful. Both series relied on the premise that Orientals and mysterious events somehow went together. Men of such background and intelligence were also considered to be particularly wise—each character had a habit of compressing philosophy and advice into weak aphorisms. But both were permitted to display wry humor. Broad comedy relief of the type already found in the Chan films eventually found its way into the newer series as well. The films in each series always left love and courtship to others of the cast. Chan was happily married with a family whose size was the subject of respectful humor; there was neither romance nor even vague hints concerning a personal life for Moto. He remained an enigma that viewers seemed to accept at face value. That meant that no continuing characters or explanatory references to unseen people were ever needed in his films. As variety in plotting caused both detectives to move freely about the world, supposedly working for Interpol or on vacation, the difference made the mysterious loner more intriguing than the wandering family man. By the final productions of the Moto series, however, even Moto had ceased to evoke much puzzlement. But the quality that most separated the two series involved a more filmic point.

Moto was a better visual character than Chan. The Chinese detective dealt exclusively with murders, committed in surroundings that required extensive use of interior sets, and he solved them by the process of quiet thought, culminating in a gathering of all the suspects to hear his findings; his Japanese counterpart handled a spectrum of crimes, permitting variety in setting and frequent use of outdoor footage, while he often donned disguises and engaged in fist fights, sometimes catching the culprits after a spectacular chase at the film's climax. In such ways Moto retained something of his agent attributes from Marquand's original thrillers. He was more the ingenious adventurer and man of action than a simple police investigator. With all their physical vitality, the Moto productions somehow seem much bigger in scope than the Chan films when in fact they are not. Viewers correctly conclude that Moto's physical prowess is quite unbelievable. The character was supposedly adept at jiu-jitsu (Lorre used a double during action scenes involving Moto) as well as at other forms of defense and weapons use. And he was always impervious to injury. Much less likely to provoke critical comment, but equally implausible, were his disguises while working under cover. They amused audiences. Apparently few viewers cared how he came to know all those facts, languages, dialects, and customs that allowed him so easily to assume special identities. Of all the ways in which the planning and packaging of the Moto productions differed from those of the Chan films, the elements designed for visual impact were indeed most noticeable.

A number of people who contributed to the conception and development of the film projects warrant special attention, for in their most effective collaborations they gave even these low-budget films a remarkably professional look and an acceptable overall quality; in other films they lent a strength to some components that helped compensate for much weaker elements. In only one or two instances did their collective efforts fail to create a product of at least some cinematic interest. Hence the achievements of scriptwriters, producers, directors, cameramen, and actors deserve specific review.

Marquand never wrote screenplays for the films featuring Moto.[7] Nor indeed were plots after the two initial productions even drawn from his stories. Scripts instead followed ideas developed by various professionals in the industry, in all but one instance as two-person collaborations, with the usual director of the series credited as the co-writer for five films.[8] Although the first two screenplays might be called adaptations because they preserved Marquand's title and very broad story lines, they became in fact almost totally new products. Director Norman Foster worked on the first with Howard Ellis Smith and on the second with Willis Cooper. The latter collaboration produced the best script, for *Thank You, Mr. Moto,* and also the premise for a subsequent offering. On three other scripts Foster worked with another writer, Philip MacDonald, who also wrote several screenplays for the Chan series. The remaining two scripts reflect special circumstances, one involving the hasty altering of a story originally intended for a different project, the other a reworking of previously used material. Yet few of the screenplays showed great imagination in conception or writing. Instead they relied on formula situations and routine treatments presented with little ingenuity or freshness. Because, in large part, of the overall mediocrity and specific weaknesses of the screenplays, later films in the series seemed rather tired efforts.

Throughout the series the production teams working on the individual films tended to include many of the same people.[9] Sol M. Wurtzel produced five of the first six films; the exception, *Mr. Moto's Gamble,* with unusual origins, was one of the two entries produced by John Stone. The last film to be released was apparently a general studio production. Foster directed six of the eight prewar films. An actor who shifted careers in his mid-thirties as starring roles disappeared, he handled the directing of the first Moto film as only his third such assignment. He quickly mastered the necessary skills and later made several respected films.[10] The two Moto films he did not direct were the Stone productions. They had James Tinling and Herbert Leeds as directors. Photography supervision for those two films fell to Lucien Andriot, one of the studio's best craftsmen, but other Moto films also had the services of top cameramen. One of those staff photographers, Virgil Miller, had responsibility for four films. Samuel Kaylin served as music director for all of the films during 1937–39. Having these and other experienced professionals on the production teams, people well accustomed to working together, gave the films good technical quality despite their tight budgets.

Hollywood casting led eventually to the permanent identification of the Moto character with Peter Lorre. The Hungarian-born actor grew up in Vienna, won early success on the stage in Berlin, achieved instant international fame on the screen in Fritz Lang's *M* (1931) by playing a tormented and frightened child-killer, left Germany for political reasons to work in England, and then in 1934 decided to try Hollywood. His first stint in the film colony left Lorre dissatisfied, however, and he soon returned to London, where opportunities seemed better.[11] Alfred Hitchcock used him there in *The Secret Agent* (1936). A reviewer of the film captured well the actor's skill and uniqueness:

> As satyr, humorist, and lethal snake, he shows, here as always, a complete feeling for the real juice of situations and the best way of distilling this through voice, carriage, motion. He is one of the true characters of the theatre, having mastered loose oddities and disfigurements until the total is a style, childlike, beautiful, unfathomably wicked, always hinting at things it would not be good to know.[12]

Armed with new success Lorre returned to Hollywood in 1936 under contract to Twentieth Century–Fox and got the Moto assignment soon afterward. At first he welcomed the role as a pleasant departure from playing psychopaths and quirky villains. Because of his own appearance, short though stocky, rather moon-faced, with protruding eyes, a distinctive voice, and accented speech, he was considered right physically. The only minor alterations required for the role involved wearing false buck teeth and unusual steel-rimmed glasses. His very youthfulness—he was in his mid-thirties when he made the films—helped suggest agelessness. Although his screen performances both before and after the series were considerably better, Lorre made the most of Moto, a part that unfortunately gave him little chance to demonstrate his full abilities. Yet without question his portrayal brought strength and appeal to the series.

Supporting actors and actresses assigned to the Moto films heightened the sense of professionalism. Drawn generally from the studio's roster of contract players, they were experienced character actors of different ages, people able to make themselves believable in their roles. There was an atmosphere of ensemble acting in the films, one of highly competent performers working together efficiently and effectively, understanding the demands and constraints of such low-budget films. The nature of the series provided more opportunities for males than females, of course, and the supporting actors appearing in it form an impressive list. Included were Sig Rumann, J. Carrol Naish, Sidney Blackmer, John Carradine, Harold Huber, Ward Bond, Lon Chaney, Jr., J. Edward Bromberg, Leon Ames, Ricardo Cortez, George Sanders, Jean Hersholt, Douglas Dumbrille, Joseph Schildkraut, Lionel Atwill, and others. Thomas Beck and Robert Lowery played romantic leads, and comedy, once added, was provided by Maxie Rosenbloom and Warren Hymer. Roles for women were more limited in number and scope. Leads fell to younger actresses—Virginia Field, Lynn Bari, Jayne Regan, Rochelle Hudson, Mary Maguire, Amanda Duff—but character roles scarcely existed. Pauline Frederick nevertheless excelled as Madame Chung in the exceptional *Thank You, Mr. Moto*. Reviewers at the time of the films' releases and observers now tend to concur that the casts represented a consistently strong feature of the series.

During the course of the principal series before World War II the quality of the individual films varied greatly. Although the best productions came at the beginning, the pattern of decline thereafter was general rather than steady, with an occasional later entry showing new strength. The following brief survey of the eight prewar films is a basic guide to their plot lines, evaluating each production by citing both concurrent and retrospective film criticism, and underscoring how the entire film sequence differed in character from the stories published in magazines and books. Greater attention has been given to the four films of unusual interest: the two purporting to use the author's original material, one derived from a Chan project that was abandoned, and especially the sole production using the espionage motif. The films in the order of their release are *Think Fast, Mr. Moto* (1937), *Thank You, Mr. Moto* (1937), *Mr. Moto's Gamble* (1938), *Mr. Moto Takes a Chance* (1938), *Mysterious Mr. Moto* (1938), *Mr. Moto's Last Warning* (1939), *Mr. Moto in Danger Island* (1939), and *Mr. Moto Takes a Vacation* (1939).[13]

Titles assigned the various Moto films are often peculiar. Each of the productions understandably used the detective's name to create instant box-office recognition by prospective viewers. But other parts of the six titles not taken from the printed stories seem to have been designed primarily to entice audiences, not to describe the films' contents. Emphasis apparently lay on words that promised viewers some sort of excitement—words like "gamble," "chance," "mysterious," "warning," and "danger." Examples show how less intriguing titles were abandoned or reserved for special markets where literalness was helpful. Thus *Mr. Moto in Danger Island* was more appealing than "Mr. Moto in Puerto Rico" and *Mr. Moto's Last Warning* had more power than "Mr. Moto in Egypt." In another instance a preliminary title included the words "Devil's Island" because they would convey a certain image to the public. Changes in titles during the production process and for different markets and releases are understandable. Yet it is difficult to find in the scripts themselves any connection to some of the final titles. They were clearly chosen for effect rather than for relevance.

Twentieth Century–Fox appears to have acquired screen rights to *No Hero* in the autumn of 1935, but no film was made from the introductory story, *No Hero*'s mixture of Japanese, Soviet, and American rivalry being too risky a subject for the Hollywood studio. It is indeed difficult to see how the material might have been reworked to preserve any of its premise or substance and yet avoid the sensitive political issues that troubled the filmmakers. Marquand's second and third stories were serialized during the early months and autumn of 1936. They became the first two films, in the sense that their titles were retained, but they were adapted in reverse order. In both scripts the original elements involving international conflict over Japan's territorial expansion were deleted and traditional crime motifs substituted.

Think Fast, Mr. Moto preserved the title and major character but little else from the third of Marquand's stories. Thus in 1937 the first Moto film set the pattern for the nearly total transformation of the leading figure and plot situations by Twentieth Century–Fox. Now Moto was no longer a Japanese intelligence agent but rather a San Francisco importer and amateur sleuth, whose self-determined responsibility is to solve several mysteries and run down a ring of gem and drug smugglers, pursuing his task aboard a ship taking the main characters from San Francisco to Shanghai. Absent from the film are the book's Honolulu setting, the gambling house, Soviet intrigue in Manchuria, the banking firm, and Moto's involvement as a representative of his government. Even the names of most characters were altered—for example, Wilson Hitchings became Bob Hitchings and was not a banker but the son of a shipping magnate. Some of the changes are understandable given the shift of media: the original plot based on secret transfers of funds was too complicated and improbable, and the young hero seemed too stuffy. But Hollywood clearly intended to have only another Oriental detective.[14] The film's technical aspects, reflecting the studio's interest in launching a successful series, were nevertheless handled skillfully. Although certainly not a major production, the film offered solid entertainment that won favorable reactions from the reviewers and public, so that additional output was planned.[15]

A sequel that followed rapidly upon the heels of the introductory production is arguably the best film of the series. *Thank You, Mr. Moto* appeared in theaters in December 1937. It kept both the title of the second Marquand story and the Peking setting but made significant changes in plot lines. Still at issue in the screen version was a set of ancient Chinese scrolls, now no longer merely art treasures but instead enhanced in value, for they collectively hold the secret of where Genghis Khan's riches lie long hidden. Prince Chung has all but one of the scrolls but surrenders them so that his mother will not be tortured by a gang led by a criminal named Kroeger. Yet the elderly woman, who regards her son's behavior as unworthy weakness, dies acting on her own. The prince then commits suicide in remorse. Moto thereupon undertakes to avenge the Chungs. When he has managed to accomplish that goal and has the precious scrolls, he respectfully destroys them all, thereby protecting the lost treasure and letting his friends face their ancestors without shame. A number of elements fused to make the film treatment effective: the carefully constructed plot, the visual background of an exciting city whose troubles were much in the news at the time, the highly competent cast, and a rousing climax with the hero and his foes fighting it out aboard a junk.[16] All that was nevertheless merely conventional material handled with considerable skill by experienced professionals. But an unusual strength lay in the delineation of the poignant relationship between the protagonist and his friends. No other Moto film allowed the depth of feeling and characterization that this production permitted Lorre to develop.

That the studio saw the series as just an economically made commercial product became still more evident in the creation of the third film. It marked a departure in that it owed nothing whatsoever to any Marquand story. *Mr. Moto's Gamble* began as a script intended for the series featuring Charlie Chan, but production had stopped with the terminal illness of Warner Oland.[17] The Chan films might well have been abandoned given the death of their star; in the end, of course, they were not. Keye Luke had meanwhile already filmed some scenes for his role as young Lee Chan. To salvage them and perhaps to supply cinemas quickly with a comparable genre film, the studio reworked the Chan script into a vehicle for its newer Oriental detective star, having him run a detective school where his rival's son has come to study. No one bothered to explain why Chan himself would not have trained the young man or why Moto found himself teaching courses in criminology. Reviewers at the time of the film's release, undoubtedly more aware of the special circumstances than the general public, noted that the film appeared to have been put together hastily, but ordinary viewers probably sensed fewer such flaws.[18] The story of murder in the boxing world had believable fight scenes and good comic relief. Much of the film's humor was supplied by a former boxing champion, Maxie Rosenbloom, who came to specialize in roles as a slightly befuddled prizefighter. This was the first Moto film with such comedy. It probably remained as a holdover from the original Chan script, where an element of broad humor was standard. But otherwise the material was familiar and the mystery itself unchallenging. A highly competent cast of character actors nevertheless made the final product seem somehow better than its weak premise and routine plot.

Yet it is doubtful that the emergency affecting the Chan films alone caused the Moto series to undergo its change of material and direction. Two points are important. Marquand had not written any further Moto adventures between the two published in 1936 and the next serialized in 1938. Thus the studio had either rejected or adapted for screen treatment the three existing stories. If the series were to continue, capitalizing on its popularity, new plots had to be devised. That the change was clearly under way before the crisis over Oland's illness is also apparent from the Moto film that had already been in preparation even before the emergency.[19] Its release so soon after the rapidly reworked Chan film and its generally weak plot and production qualities all suggest that both change and decline in the Moto series had been likely even without the unexpected situation.

Mr. Moto Takes a Chance appeared in late spring 1938, only two months after *Mr. Moto's Gamble.* Despite the fact that four different writers devised its plot lines, two providing the original story and two others the final screenplay, the story relied heavily on the implausible and melodramatic.[20] In many ways the film merely borrowed from other familiar types, combining a setting in an exotic jungle state, standard notions of simple natives being misled into rebellion, and the saving heroics of friendly foreign agents, but it lacked the essential element of genuine intrigue or mystery. A local ruler of uncertain nationality, played by J. Edward Bromberg, needs help when a priest plans an insurrection. For some vague reason Moto and a beautiful Western agent must become involved. The hero and his unlikely counterpart, portrayed by Rochelle Hudson, foil the uprising and save the monarch's throne. Reviewers justly criticized nearly every aspect of the production except its unfortunate performers.[21] In speculating on exactly where the story supposedly took place, mentioning both Indochina and Sumatra as possibilities, they noted in particular how cheap and unconvincing the sets were. B. R. Crisler thought that the locale purported to be Indochina but that "indoor China would be a more accuate description" of the sets provided by Twentieth Century–Fox.[22] Aside from the experienced cast, there was indeed little to recommend to film, the fourth in the series. Moto films had clearly sunk to the level of the routine B's.

Mysterious Mr. Moto represented a slight improvement over *Mr. Moto Takes a Chance*. Fifth in the series and the third Moto film released in 1938, it benefitted from a better story and greater care in production, Foster seeming more comfortable with the London background than with false jungles. Yet all the studio work must have been rushed, for the completed film appeared in theaters soon after its predecessor, and it was noticeably short for a feature film. The plot begins with Moto serving a penal sentence on Devil's Island in order to gain the confidence of a fellow prisoner whom Moto then helps to escape to Great Britain to rejoin his gang. Moto is, of course, with Interpol. He prevents a ring of notorious international criminals from killing an inventor and stealing his formula for a new industrial process. Despite a story line already familiar to film audiences, the handling of the London underworld atmosphere and assortment of rather Dickensian figures has visual appeal, and both direction and performances showed a flair.[23] Thus the film offered the type of popular entertainment it and the series were intended to provide.

Careful plotting and another strong cast gave the next release, *Mr. Moto's Last Warning* (January 1939), a timeliness and overall quality that helped sustain the series. This sixth film in the sequence is especially noteworthy because its makers not only returned to a situation involving major world events but also took a stand with respect to key ideological issues of the period. Yet in doing so they were careful to show Moto as a man of peace operating far from home. Thus the film could deal with international conflict without having the title character identified with his own nation's increasingly aggressive policy. The participation of a solid ensemble of actors and actresses, many with recognizable names and well-deserved reputations for supporting work, also accounts for the production's high ranking among the series entries. Despite such merits, the film remained a B product destined to be shown in double billings.

Posing as a quiet dealer in Oriental art and antiques but really an agent working with the Interpol organization, Moto must investigate reports of a possible international incident in Egypt, one the perpetrators hope will cause France to break its friendship with Britain and further the gang's ambitions. They plan to blow up warships of the French fleet and make Britain appear to bear responsibility for the outrage. Moto's task is to identify and eliminate the danger before the ships reach Port Said for strategically vital and well-publicized joint maneuvers with the British. Having the hero work against such an impending deadline builds an element of dramatic suspense into the story that greatly enhances its appeal.

Action begins aboard a passenger ship bound for Port Said with George Sanders easily identified by viewers as a suave villain. He befriends a French admiral's wife in hope of learning exactly when her husband's fleet will reach Egypt for the exercises. Also aboard is a young man calling himself Moto, who is murdered soon after the ship docks, but not before the real Moto has conferred with him. The writer's introduction of this confusing false Moto is an imaginative and intriguing plotting device that relies upon audiences' awareness of Moto's love of disguises to outwit his opponents. In the next important scene the leaders of the conspiracy, who recognize each other by a Maltese cross printed on matchbook covers, are gathered in a dressing room of a variety theater. Ricardo Cortez is appearing there as a ventriloquist known as Fabian the Great. He warns the others in the ring he heads that no one must discover what nation they serve. But Moto has managed to listen to their conversation from another room and narrowly escapes from the building disguised as a bearded French juggler. When Cortez realizes from seeing an old photograph that John Carradine, who has succeeded in penetrating the gang, is really a British secret service agent, he plans to kill Carradine at an opportune moment. Moto has also realized the man's true identity, for they had met in Nepal some two years earlier, and he learns more about the gang from him. Nevertheless, Cortez soon succeeds in disposing of the unsuspecting Carradine.

Moto's shop stands opposite a small hotel and bar run by Virginia Field that serves as headquarters for the sabotage ring led by Cortez.

Field's suspicions that her lover is more than a variety artist are temporarily allayed by Cortez's story that he is really a smuggler. He then asks her to follow Moto because he now believes that the overly inquisitive art and antique dealer is the true Moto. She learns that the shopkeeper has shown interest in a salvage ship supposedly working on a wreck near the entrance to the Suez Canal. Cortez had actually arranged the sinking so that the salvage ship could secretly lay mines to blow up a visiting warship and perhaps block the canal approach. But Field overhears Sanders report that the fleet is due the next day and is shocked to learn the real nature of Cortez's activities. Meanwhile Cortez has failed in an effort to kill Moto because the agent spotted the bomb in his shop and threw it out a window.

As the final showdown draws near, Moto's hope that a rather silly English writer and tourist, Robert Coote, will bring the Egyptian police ends when Sanders intercepts him, luring him to the gang's pier. There both he and Moto, who is subdued after a rousing fight, are tied in weighted bags and thrown into the water to drown, although the resourceful agent frees himself and then saves Coote. Field has remained an English patriot despite her shady life and is knocked out while trying to summon the Egyptian authorities to stop Cortez. The climax comes the next morning. As the fleet approaches Sanders slips underwater to detonate the mines upon receiving a signal from Cortez; Moto dives into the sea to stop him and the explosions occur prematurely as Sanders is overpowered. Moto then confronts Cortez on the dock, appearing to be losing a fist fight, until Field shows up and shoots Cortez. The film ends quickly as the gang is arrested and the heroes take stock of their success.[24]

Conceptual and technical components of the production were especially well handled. The film illustrates how simply a team working in a studio can create an aura of intrigue and excitement by the skillful combining of suggestive allusions and cumulative detail: references to important naval maneuvers, exotic Port Said, and protecting the Suez Canal; the presence of danger from clever foreign agents and saboteurs using secret recognition codes; visual interest achieved through shifting of scenes among unusual and colorful backgrounds; the complication over a false Moto, Moto in disguise, and Moto repeatedly in trouble. Set design and special lighting effects allowed the photography to convey a strong sense of local atmosphere and dark brooding mystery. For contrasts in texture and mood there were insertions of newsreel footage showing ships in fleet formation, comic relief drawing upon the broad humor of Coote's portrayal of a fussy and awkward young man, and several scenes in which the hero must engage in physical struggles with each of the villains. Entirely absent from the action-oriented film, however, were any elements of love or romance. With its plot well paced in both direction and editing, and with a cast of experienced performers taking pride in their craft, the film overcame nearly all the problems of budgetary constraints.

Hurried production nevertheless led to curious oversights. In his minimal disguise as a rather scholarly art dealer Lorre wore dark-framed glasses, but he neither lost nor broke them during a lengthy fight sequence, and both he and Coote surfaced wearing their glasses after the attempt to drown them. In another scene the man planting the bomb in the shop easily enters a window in a storage room—something scarcely believable at premises filled with valuable art objects in a city notorious for its crime rate. And more skeptical viewers might also question just how Moto established himself so quickly as a local art dealer. The need to detonate the mines from underwater is similarly contrived; its purpose is merely to allow a different kind of struggle there. Nor at any point is the meaning of "last warning" in the title made clear to the audience. The words appear to have had only a good box-office appeal. But these are minor flaws in an enjoyable if unpretentious piece of entertainment.

Probably the most significant aspect of the film is its political content. The screenplay developed by Foster and Philip MacDonald, who collaborated on three scripts for the series, gives evidence of Hollywood's new anti-Axis stand. Studios had hitherto generally shied away from controversial positions in international affairs. Some caution over market sensitivities also lingered here, for the identity of the nation behind the plot is never revealed to the viewers, although the actors show surprise upon learning it. But even without naming the scheming enemy power, the filmmakers left little doubt as to its likely identity, since audiences knew which nations opposed the democracies. Fascist Italy had long been pursuing a policy of aggressive expansion in the Mediterranean region, making it the more probable culprit, since Nazi Germany had not yet shown much interest in naval strategy or the Middle East. But clearly one of the Axis powers was the unnamed plotter. Basing the story so firmly on contemporary world tensions gave the production far more substance than its immediate predecessors in the series had possessed. Yet this venture into serious international politics was apparently considered too risky and was not pursued in either of the two remaining prewar productions.

For the final Moto film to be produced—but not the last of the series in terms of release to theaters—the studio retailored the plot of a 1934 film.[25] In the process the material lost much of its believability. The result was that *Mr. Moto in Danger Island* had only limited appeal. For some unexplained reason, Moto has been hired by the United States government to investigate a diamond-smuggling operation in Puerto Rico that has already cost one American agent his life. The detective must identify and apprehend the guilty parties in order to remove suspicion from honest but helpless officials. He accomplishes his task with more than the usual number of chases and fights and with some rather broad humor supplied by an assistant.[26] It is impossible to say whether such elements might have become permanent characteristics of the series had it continued. They gave the film a certain vitality, and the skilled cast managed to minimize the effect of the plot's unlikely premise and lack of genuine mystery, but the production offered nothing more than standard fare for double billings.

Mr. Moto Takes a Vacation actually predated *Mr. Moto in Danger Island.* Yet the film was not released until about eight months after its completion and three months after distribution of the later production.[27] No specific reason for the delay is known. The film possesses no real merit, and studio interest in the series had waned. It was the third Moto film released in the first seven months of 1939 and last of the series. Nothing about it, except the professionalism of the cast, shows careful effort. The plot involving an international jewel robbery is confused, sets and props seem unusually shoddy, lighting and camera work are uninspired, and the direction lacks clarity of purpose and pace.[28] Everyone appeared to be so tired of the whole project that some reviewers could not resist playing upon the title. The *New York Times* critic said Moto was not on vacation, "He just seems to be missing on several cylinders," and concluded that, "In short, the fairest thing one can say for 'Mr. Moto Takes a Vacation' is that, in this case, it would have been a swell idea."[29] Apparently the public and the studio agreed. Moto films were terminated in 1939.[30]

The reasons for the discontinuation of the Moto series include a number of production problems. It is therefore a misconception to attribute the decision to curtail the films solely to growing anti-Japanese feeling on the eve of World War II. Lorre had already tired of the Moto character and was eager to revitalize his career by undertaking roles that were more varied and demanding. During the run of the Moto series he made only one other film, a poorly received comedy, and appeared in a second comedy in 1940 to fulfill his expiring contract. Thereafter he won supporting parts in films of high quality, notably *The Maltese Falcon* in 1941 and *Casablanca* in 1942, working as an independent agent at different studios.[31] Lorre nevertheless found himself portraying only rather stereotypical characters until his death in 1964.

Another important factor in the termination of the Moto films was the decline of the series format. Low-budget productions intended primarily for double-feature showings had been losing their box-office appeal as film audiences became more sophisticated and prosperous. The exhaustion of formulas, characterizations, and ideas was obvious. Major studios announced that they were dropping all but a few of the most successful series.[32] Moto was retained initially, but his eventual disappearance predated that of Chan.[33] Alternatives to cancellation were dismissed as costly and unwarranted. Fuller development and humanization of the title character might have kept audiences more interested; another actor could have been substituted, as was done in the Chan films, with a minimal amount of reaction; tighter plotting and better direction might have enhanced the elements of intrigue and suspense. But the series was not considered worth such efforts.[34] At the same time it must be noted that Twentieth Century–Fox did not relinquish its rights to the character as it had done with the Chan films, which continued at a lesser studio. It is only at this point that possible audience rejection of the focal character on political or nationalist grounds became decisive.

Film scholars who cite only anti-Japanese sentiment as the reason for discontinuing the Moto films have therefore oversimplified the situation. Hollywood may well have been more sensitive to perceptions or fears of altered attitudes in the mass market than a subscription magazine like *Collier's*. Yet the fact that the latter published a Moto story as much as two years after the last Moto film suggests that other factors cannot be ignored. Certainly a combination of considerations, understandably including anxiety over growing American resentment of Japan's trade policies and expansionist activities, accounts for the disappearance of the series.

Two postwar Hollywood films must also be examined to complete discussion of the cinematic treatment of Marquand's character. One holds special interest as a further striking example of how filmmakers adapted the writer's material for their own purposes with little respect for the integrity of its original content. It was Hollywood's version of the final novel in which Moto appeared. The second film reportedly represented an attempt, perhaps none too serious, to introduce a new continuing series. There were no further productions, however, after the initial weak effort.

In 1957 Twentieth Century–Fox released its adaptation of Marquand's *Stopover: Tokyo*. The film version of the last Moto novel achieved an ultimate in transformation by omitting entirely the Japanese agent from its cast and script. Although the film's creators retained Marquand's original title—without the colon—they must have felt Moto's image was undesirable. Attracted by the story's suitability for a major color production with prominent stars, the filmmakers apparently feared that anything identifiable as "a Moto film" would suggest to prospective viewers the wrong connotations, recalling the old mystery and detective films made on cost-cutting production budgets. So in their script collaboration producer Walter Reisch and director Richard Breen reworked the story material rather extensively. Yet in one basic respect their interpretation remained faithful to the novel: it preserved the essentials of a thriller involving dangerous international intrigue.

An American counterintelligence agent played by Robert Wagner must somehow block an attempt by Communist conspirators led by fellow countryman Edmond O'Brien to assassinate the ambassador to Japan. His task presents added difficulties because the intended victim refuses to realize his danger or cooperate in matters of security. But the plotters' scheme to kill him during the dedication of a peace monument, thereby threatening American-Japanese political ties, fails when the hero at last manages to discover and dispose of the bomb.[35] Embodied in the film's handling of this relatively simple story line were attitudes that now seem rather naïve and old-fashioned. During the postwar period Hollywood had become willing to depict espionage and terrorist activities carried out by agents and traitors alike who seemed to be Americans of quite ordinary types. But all espionage activities, regardless of their importance or aims, still carried a stigma. In this instance the hero has been romancing a young woman, Joan Collins, who turns him down when she learns of his profession. The views expressed by the ambassador and the girl reflect the traditional values of a world different from that in which the agent and the Communist agitator both live.

Stopover Tokyo appeared in color and CinemaScope. The film used beautiful Japanese locations and cultural associations to good effect, often tied to a subplot involving custody of a small child, but it might just as readily have been set in Argentina or elsewhere. Without Moto it had become a movable tale of Americans abroad. Worst of all, the film moves slowly. With a running time of an hour and forty minutes, it prolongs an uncomplicated plot to the point where the excitement so necessary to a thriller no longer prevails, dissipated by travelogue-type footage and too many incidentals. The production may be admired for its handsome qualities but must be criticized for its thin plot and pedestrian pace.[36]

A rather curious attempt to revive the Moto character in a film released in 1965 had little to commend it to audiences. *The Return of Mr. Moto* nevertheless shows that legal rights to the name had been retained by Twentieth Century–Fox. Undoubtedly intended to capitalize on the great popularity of the new James Bond series, the production was uninspired in both concept and quality, although Twentieth Century–Fox reportedly hoped to build another series around the famous figure. The film's poor reception by critics and public alike ended any such plans. On this occasion Moto, portrayed by Henry Silva, again represents Interpol, combatting crime in London. A syndicate of international schemers has planned to assassinate Middle East oil producers and then take control of all their holdings. The plot lacked originality, and the film's low production standards caused it to suffer badly in comparison with others in the rash of slick espionage and adventure thrillers being released about the same time. And Silva as Moto looked even less Japanese than Lorre had.[37] Everything about the film suggests that it was prepared hurriedly to take advantage of a market trend. That no sequel ever appeared is scarcely surprising.

Twentieth Century–Fox followed a businesslike course in handling its Moto film rights in the period from autumn 1935 through 1939. It avoided controversial content and tapped a prepared market. Unwilling to risk using the original stories' mix of international crises and espionage, the studio modified the character and his adventures to fit a conventional crime and action mold, while waiting until magazine publication of three adventures had built name recognition. Having then departed so far from the author's concept and plots in the first two productions, and having exhausted his available material, the filmmakers created their own screenplays, deciding correctly that the favorable audience reception of the initial films would sustain a longer series.

Not all of the continuing series from those years fell into the B classification, but this one was openly geared to that mass market— although Moto films did begin with quality that was above the average for their category. There is evidence that their subsequent decline would have set in earlier had the problem with the Chan project not caused a change in the studio's production priorities and created a comparatively strong third film. But the next two Moto films were more typical of the many B-level products being made. Although changing market conditions by 1939 led major studios to cancel many of their series, this sequence was still profitable enough to be retained, and it is possible that the strength of the sixth Moto film influenced the decision. *Mr. Moto's Last Warning,* as the sole espionage and sabotage story of the series, also comes closest to the spirit of Marquand's Moto. But it was followed by a film using a reworked old screenplay, certainly more solid than another production actually completed somewhat earlier but not released immediately, but a remarkably tired effort that ended the series on an unfortunate note. Despite their low budgets and occasional weaknesses, most of the films were good entertainment for patrons of the nation's many neighborhood theaters.

The belief that the central character's Japanese background and identity account for the discontinuation of the Moto series is popular but not fully accurate. Little point was made in the films about his national origin, and as an international detective he never directly served his own country. Perhaps more important reasons for the studio's decision were its analyses of a declining interest in serials, its restive star, and its unwillingness to commit more money and talent to a project that scarcely warranted such investment. The series had been commercially successful but had outlived its usefulness.

1. See Douglas W. Churchill, "Hollywood Calls the Shadow and His Pals," *The New York Times*, 23 May 1937, reprinted in *The New York Times Encyclopedia of Film.*

2. Twentieth Century-Fox was formed in May 1935 by the merger of the troubled Fox Film Corporation and the production company called Twentieth Century Pictures that Darryl F. Zanuck and Joseph M. Schenck had founded in 1933. See "The Studio and the Men Who Made It" in Tony Thomas and Aubrey Solomon, *The Films of 20th Century-Fox: A Pictorial History* (rev. ed.; Secaucus, N.J.: The Citadel Press, 1985), pp. 11–22. The Charlie Chan series had begun at Fox Films in 1931. Its characteristics and history are discussed later in other connections.

3. It is noteworthy that the Moto series is usually listed by film scholars as part of the detective film genre and not as belonging to Hollywood's output of spy pictures. Only *Mr. Moto's Last Warning* is listed in "463 Great Spy Pictures" in James R. Parish and Michael R. Pitts, *The Great Spy Pictures* (Metuchen, N.J.: The Scarecrow Press, Inc., 1974), pp. 43–524 (especially pp. 304–5). Nor is the Moto series even mentioned in the authors' "History of the Spy Film" on pp. 9–42.

4. Chan films also spawned other variations in the 1930s. In 1938 Monogram Pictures launched a series based on Hugh Wiley's Mr. Wong character from stories in *Collier's*. Boris Karloff played Wong in the first five films; the final production in 1940 starred Keye Luke. See William K. Everson, *The Detective in Film* (Secaucus, N.J.: The Citadel press, 1972), p. 82, and Michael R. Pitts, *Famous Movie Detectives* (Metuchen, N.J.: The Scarecrow Press, Inc., 1979), pp. 207–13. The series ended at a time when many such series were being dropped. See the discussion concerning the termination of the Moto series.

5. For example, in describing *The Return of Mr. Moto*, a 1965 film attempting to revive the character, two respected film scholars expressed some surprise that the detective had been made into a James Bond–type figure. In fact, the 1965 characterization was closer to that in the original stories than the detective image of most prewar Moto films had been. See Parish and Pitts, p. 392.

6. There are good discussions of both characters in chapter 7, "The Oriental Detectives," of Everson, pp. 72–85, and in chapter 3, "Charlie Chan," and chapter 9, "Mr. Moto," in Pitts, pp. 39–84 and 195–205, respectively.

7. One biographer says he did submit "new scripts" to the studio with titles like "Mr. Moto in the Persian Oil Fields" (Bell, p. 249). There is no evidence that any of his ideas or proposals were ever used. He was not credited with story suggestions or development for any of the films after the first two.

8. Of the eight writers who worked on the Moto scripts in addition to Norman Foster, none appears to have been highly experienced. Nor does any of them seem to have gone on to greater success in film-writing later. See Larry Langman, *A Guide to American Screenwriters: The Sound Era, 1929–1982* (2 vols.; New York: Garland Publishing, Inc., 1984).

9. The filmography identifies the principal members of the production staff and cast for each film. Note that some performers also appeared in more than one film.

10. Foster had first appeared on the screen in 1928. His seven-year marriage to Claudette Colbert ended in 1935, and in 1936 he decided to try directing. But for a while he also continued to take smaller roles in films. *Journey into Fear,* one of his best achievements as a director, was made at RKO in 1943. See David Ragan, *Who's Who in Hollywood, 1900–1976* (New Rochelle, N.Y.: Arlington House, Publishers, Inc., 1976), p. 147, and James R. Parish and Michael R. Pitts, *Film Directors: A Guide to Their American Films* (Metuchen, N.J.: The Scarecrow Press, Inc., 1974), pp. 137–38.

11. Born Laszlo Loewenstein on 26 June 1904, Lorre began his career in theater in 1924; he left Germany because of the Nazis. A good summary of Lorre's early career appears in Ted Sennett, *Masters of Menace: Greenstreet and Lorre* (New York: E. P. Dutton & Co., 1979), pp. 3–39.

12. Otis Ferguson, review, quoted by Sennett, p. 36. Lorre always had trouble fighting the tendency to cast him as a sinister figure after his role in *M.*

13. Synopses and comments on all the pre-war Moto films may be found in Stephen D. Youngkin et al., *The Films of Peter Lorre* (Secaucus, N.J.: The Citadel Press, 1982). Prints of the prewar films are now difficult to find because the productions were not considered significant enough at the time to be preserved or collected. Even the major film archives have incomplete holdings. But the films are in public domain and are still shown occasionally on television by independent stations or cable networks filling their broadcasting schedules with old motion pictures. Such prints are likely to be imperfect. Only *Mr. Moto's Last Warning* is currently available on videocassette. See James J. Mulay et al., eds., *Spies and Sleuths: Mystery, Spy and Suspense Films on Videocassette* (Evanston, Ill.: CineBooks, Inc., 1988).

14. See the earlier discussion of the book for details of how the film differed from its source. For additional flavor, a beautiful Oriental girl played by Lotus Long was added in the screenplay. But in none of the films was any romantic involvement planned for the detective.

15. Only a limited selection of the contemporary reviews may be noted. Citations for reviews from *Variety* and the *New York Times* refer to published collections of such articles: *Variety Film Reviews,* volumes for 1934–37, 1938–42, and 1954–58 (New York: Garland Publishing, Inc., 1983), and *The New York Times Film Reviews,* volumes 2–4 (New York: The New York Times and Arno Press, 1970). Since both collections are organized chronologically, the date of the review is the key to its location, but the latter source is also paginated, so that those citations also include both volume and page numbers. The reviews in *Variety* were not signed. Review in *Variety,* 18 August 1937; John T. McManus, review, 16 August 1937, *New York Times* 2, 1418; Pitts, pp. 196–97; Thomas and Solomon, p. 59.

16. Review in *Variety,* 12 January 1938; B. R. Crisler, review, 3 January 1938, *New York Times* 2, 1461; Pitts, p. 197; Sennett, pp. 39–40.

17. Warner Oland became unable to continue work in January 1938. By then the studio had invested about $100,000 in the project. See *Time*, 28 March 1938, p. 38. A final title for the Chan film had apparently not been chosen before Oland became ill and later died. The aborted project is known by several titles: *Charlie Chan at the Fights, Charlie Chan at the Ringside, Charlie Chan at the Arena*.

18. Review in *Variety*, 13 April 1938; Bosley Crowther, review, 8 April 1938, *New York Times* 2, 1488; Thomas and Solomon, p. 74; Pitts, pp. 41–42, 49, 198.

19. That the film was started before the crisis arose over Oland's health in early 1938 is confirmed by a reviewer who saw it in production. It obviously underwent various changes before completion. Douglas Churchill reported his impressions upon seeing the film being made in August 1937. It was then being called *Look Out, Mr. Moto* and had Sally Blane listed as the female lead. Neither the crew nor the cast seemed to be taking their assignments very seriously. In Churchill's estimation it was clearly intended to be a B film. Douglas W. Churchill, "Cleaning and Blocking Hollywood's Old Hat," *New York Times*, 22 August 1937, reprinted in *The New York Times Encyclopedia of Film*. Sally Blane had married Norman Foster in the mid-1930s. Both were involved in later Chan films.

20. Norman Foster and Willis Cooper, who collaborated on the screenplay for the successful *Thank You, Mr. Moto*, are credited with the idea for *Mr. Moto Takes a Chance*, which Foster directed, but the screenplay was written by Lou Breslow and John Patrick, the only Moto film for which they prepared a script.

21. Review in *Variety*, 13 June 1938; Crisler, review, 13 June 1938, *New York Times*, 2, 1507. See also Thomas and Solomon, p. 74, and Pitts, p. 199.

22. Crisler, review, 13 June 1938, *New York Times* 2, 1507.

23. Reviews in *Variety*, 1 June and 21 September 1938; Thomas and Solomon, pp. 74–75. An alternative longer title, *Mysterious Mr. Moto of Devil's Island*, was apparently also used. Pitts errs in attributing the plot to a novel by Marquand. The point is discussed in a later note since it also involves the next film in the series. See Pitts, p. 199.

24. Review in *Variety*, 25 January 1939; Thomas M. Pryor, review, 27 January 1939, *New York Times* 3, 1573; Thomas and Solomon, p. 89; Pitts, p. 199; Parish and Pitts, *The Great Spy Pictures*, pp. 304–5. *Mr. Moto's Last Warning* is the only film in the prewar series given a capsule profile by Parish and Pitts. Sometimes an alternative title, *Mr. Moto in Egypt*, identifies this series entry. The generally reliable Pitts is in error with respect to this film in his study of Hollywood's detective characters. He attributes the story to a Marquand novel called *Mr. Moto's Last Warning* and says another Moto film entitled *The Mysterious Mr. Moto* was also based on the book. There was no such novel. See Pitts, p. 199. It is possible but unlikely that the films came from ideas suggested by Marquand.

25. A book by John W. Vandercook called *Murder in Trinidad: A Case in the Career of Bertram Lynch* provided the film's base. John Reinhardt and George Bricker also worked on story development, but the script for *Mr. Moto in Danger Island* was by Peter Milne. In 1934 there had been a film production

based on the story called *Murder in Trinidad* and in 1945 another version was made in which the title became *Caribbean Mystery*. The Moto film is sometimes called just *Danger Island*. See Pitts, pp. 199–200.

26. Ibid.; review in *Variety*, 22 March 1939; Crowther, review, 20 March 1939, *New York Times* 3, 1589; Thomas and Solomon, p. 89.

27. *Variety* indicated that the film was released in November 1938, but other publications cite a date in mid-1939. Films were sometimes given only a limited release or were withdrawn after an initial release. There is no readily available information concerning what happened in this instance.

28. Review in *Variety*, 16 November 1938; Crisler, review, 19 June 1939, *New York Times* 3, 1615–16; Pitts, p. 200; Thomas and Solomon, p. 89; Everson, p. 80.

29. Crisler, review, 19 June 1939, *New York Times* 3, 1615–16.

30. By that time public recognition of the character had become so great that a delightful satire of it appeared in the form of an animated cartoon. In 1939 Warner Brothers had Porky Pig play Moto in *Porky's Movie Mystery*. Detective Porky discovers that a madman terrorizing Hollywood is none other than the extraordinary Hugh Herbert. See Everson, p. 82.

31. Lorre's non-Moto films at Twentieth Century–Fox were *I'll Give a Million* in 1938 and *I Was an Adventuress* in 1940. His role in *The Maltese Falcon* took him back to the type of mentally disturbed or sinister characters he had portrayed initially and in Hitchcock's English suspense films. He worked at nearly half a dozen different studios during his later years. Sennett, pp. 40–50.

32. Studios dropped both old and new series as the market changed. Churchill reported on Hollywood's problems with series in the *New York Times* at the beginning of 1939. Lack of box-office support had caused Twentieth Century–Fox to cancel four of its seven series. He noted that the Moto and Chan films would be kept. Yet both disappeared before long. Consistently low production budgets, an essential part of every studio's approach to its series, helped destroy audience interest. Only a few series like the "Thin Man" and the "Hardy Family" films got much money to spend. Churchill, "Mr. Goldwyn Storms the 'Heights,'" *New York Times*, 8 January 1939, reprinted in *The New York Times Encyclopedia of Film*.

33. The Chan films were perhaps the most durable Hollywood series. Even they had troubles. Twentieth Century–Fox made twenty-seven Chan films during 1931–42. Warner Oland portrayed the character in sixteen films until his death in 1938; Sidney Toler then assumed the title role for eleven more films until 1942. The studio discontinued the series that year. Monogram Pictures revived the films in 1944 and after Toler's death in 1947 made six films starring Roland Winters. Never a major studio with ample funds, Monogram nevertheless earned respect for the quality of its B films, all aspects of which showed considerable care. See Everson, pp. 73–80.

34. Perhaps further evidence of the troubles confronting all series was a later script proposal for a super-mystery featuring the detectives from four studio series. *The Four Star Murder Case* was considered by Twentieth Century–Fox in 1942. It would have required the combined talents of Moto, Philo Vance, Chan, and Michael Shayne to solve a killing in an isolated mansion. Twen-

tieth Century–Fox never made the film for reasons unrelated to the Japanese Moto. Ibid., pp. 77–79.

35. See the discussion of the Marquand novel for complete story differences. In brief, the novel involves a much broader communist conspiracy, has a male and female pair of American agents working together as a team, and makes the assassination target a local political leader. Because no Japanese have essential roles in the film plot there was no reason for including anyone as important as the Moto character. The locale as far as the basic script was concerned might easily have been shifted to any part of the globe. Bell, p. 403, errs in saying Moto made his last screen appearance in 1957, for she must have been unaware how Hollywood changed the content of *Stopover: Tokyo.*

36. Reviewers who were familiar with the Marquand novel and Moto's role expressed disappointment at his absence. They often found the film's script and characterizations inconsistent with its efforts at realism. One critic called the hero "highly efficient, sartorially splendid and thoroughly implausible." Milton Esterow, review, 27 December 1957, *New York Times* 4, 3032. See also reviews in *Variety,* 30 October 1957, and *Newsweek,* 25 November 1957, p. 122, as well as Thomas and Solomon, p. 291.

37. For further critical comment on the film see Parish and Pitts, *The Great Spy Pictures,* pp. 392–93; Thomas and Solomon, pp. 355–56; Everson, p. 82; Pitts, p. 201. Silva was of Puerto Rican background and usually played villains or Latin types in Hollywood. He was in his mid-thirties when he portrayed the character.

Conclusion

A study of the Moto stories has twofold value. For students of twentieth-century popular culture it provides the first detailed inquiry concerning a famous character, the wily intelligence agent featured in six highly successful magazine serials and subsequent books, and the likable detective hero of eight film productions that avoided the printed works' focus on espionage. To the controversy that has long existed over Marquand's place in literature the study adds further dimension by calling attention to a body of his work generally overlooked by Marquand's biographers and those dealing with his major fiction. A review of some of the significant points that emerge from this study therefore gives a more accurate perspective on the author and his varied work.

Marquand never overcame the critical repercussions of his concentration on lucrative magazine fiction during the fifteen years before publication of his first major novel in 1937. His attempt thereafter to continue with such commercial output while also producing serious works, his willingness to allow some of even his best novels to be abridged and serialized, his outspoken defense of his magazine background and the skills he felt such writing required, and his prominence in the profession all tended to prolong or exacerbate his problems. To many critics and reviewers his writing always carried the stigmas of shallowness and popularity; to the author himself it represented careful craftsmanship and sound achievement in a competitive field. Even when a run of solid novels won a large readership and some grudging critical acceptance, he remained a controversial figure, a writer who clung to his conviction that working well at two levels was professionally possible. Unlike others who have tried the same approach, he never satisfied his many critics, and his reputation was hurt by his persistence. The Moto stories inevitably played a large role in the debate over the evaluation of all Marquand's work.[1]

To understand the author's commitment and loyalty to his one sustained popular fiction series, we must recognize at least four insights derived from his personal life. Marquand clearly had a love of romantic adventure that manifested itself in both his travels and his genuine enjoyment in creating stories like those about Moto. He found plotting such light tales to be mentally relaxing; the actual writing was quickly accomplished with ease and sureness. A second element in his attachment to commercially marketable fiction was his lifelong concern or anxiety over financial security. Marquand's frequent complaints that he wanted to move away from magazine work were belied by his inability on many occasions to refuse the high payments that magazines could offer him. The influence and arguments of his longtime literary agent must be considered as a third and related element. There is no doubt that the writer was deeply disturbed by the conflicting efforts of those around him to shape his career and especially by pressures for magazine fiction exerted by Brandt. Yet the agent can scarcely be cast as some sort of villain who forced a powerless or unwilling writer to turn out nothing but facile stories and serials. The fourth point concerning the Moto stories in particular is their close connection with Marquand's two marriages and their breakdown. Both the first and last of the novels owed their existence to generous magazine offers consciously made to let the writer escape his domestic problems. And the woman who became his longtime mistress, the wife of the author's agent, helped prepare the typescripts of those two stories. Thus some knowledge of Marquand's private world and circumstances also helps put the Moto novels into a personal framework.

Marquand never claimed any literary distinction for his stories about Moto. He knew and readily acknowledged the difference between literature and fiction. Yet the six espionage mysteries possess qualities in their conception and execution that give them both intrinsic merit and durable appeal. Their occasional weaknesses tend to be those common to the adventure genre: situations and complications in which romance and suspense temporarily obscure the unlikelihood or implausibility of the action, events paced so rapidly that opportunities for detail or description remain limited, and characters portrayed so stereotypically that their lack of depth appears not to matter. But Marquand prided himself on doing even formulaic work well and rarely failed to maintain the highest levels of good craftsmanship and skillful writing in his Moto books. In some matters he excelled: his ability to recall and convey the rich atmosphere of his Chinese backgrounds, his exceptional readability stemming from the clarity of his polished prose style, his pervasive theme of self-discovery through meeting challenges and accepting life, his ingenuity in creating the intriguing but not totally sympathetic Moto character. The espionage professional of the books resembles but should not be mistaken for the sanitized and bland international detective of the films. All the novels in the series remain solid entertainment decades after they were written. A few even offer more subtle satisfactions to the perceptive reader.

The answer to the question of whether Marquand broke any new ground in the field of espionage mysteries with his Moto novels must in the main be negative. He was an accomplished practitioner rather than a true innovator. Yet his handling of details showed a sense of realism. In this respect it is helpful to compare Marquand's spy stories with works by Eric Ambler that also appeared in the late 1930s. The two bodies of work have many similarities and common qualities.[2] Because Ambler's early novels are more fully and subtly developed, they have gained recognition as seminal works of the new realism in spy fiction, a position neither merited by nor accorded to Marquand's stories.[3] Yet both authors set their plots against backgrounds of contemporary events and used the premise of an innocent person becoming somehow caught up in international intrigue and espionage. Ambler's innovations are deservedly credited with setting the tone and direction of the genre's subsequent development during and after World War II. It does not detract from his accomplishment and position to suggest that Marquand also deserves a place in the ranks of pioneers in realistic spy fiction. The somber *Stopover: Tokyo* in particular helped strengthen the trend later enlarged and popularized by John Le Carré and others.

Throughout his lifetime and since his death in 1960 the debate over Marquand's stature as a writer has continued without resolution. The six Moto books form an important part of his output; although certainly not as significant as his major novels, they possess merits that justify regarding them with respect, however they may be invoked in arguments over Marquand's other works. Marquand always applied his considerable powers and talents—inquisitiveness, observation, analysis, craftsmanship, imagination, versatility—in conceiving and developing his adventures for Moto. Even those who already know and value his serious novels, but who may dismiss as unimportant his lighter fiction, will find kindred insights and unifying threads throughout the series. The great popularity of the stories and their title character over the years attests to the author's skill and lasting achievement.

NOTES

1. Two examples of how some detractors tied the Moto stories to their criticisms of Marquand's work in general suggest the types of connections. John Lardner wrote in *The New Yorker* concerning *B. F.'s Daughter:*

> Marquand's talent in his novels is exactly the same he applied in his earlier potboiling, highly successful *Saturday Evening Post* stories about Mr. Moto, the Japanese solver of crimes. That is a talent for finding and using over and over again a formula that will entertain a public accustomed to formulas.

The New Yorker, 9 November 1946, p. 117. Lardner's reference to Moto as a "solver of crimes" indicates his unfamiliarity with the content of Marquand's printed stories. Jacques Barzun and Wendell H. Taylor called the Moto books "run-of-the-mill adventure" tales written "before the author became a semi-serious novelist." *A Catalogue of Crime* (New York: Harper & Row, Publishers, 1971), p. 308. Such remarks reveal how the Moto stories provided a basis for unfavorable linkage of Marquand's light fiction and his major novels. The charge that all the author's writing adhered to basic formulas has been common. See also Leo Gurko, "The High Level Formula of J. P. Marquand," *American Scholar* 21 (October 1952), 443–53. One of the more sympathetic analyses of how Marquand's popular and serious fiction is interrelated may be found in Gross, pp. 7, 21, passim. A fuller development of similar ideas appears in Clifton Fadiman's introduction to the anthology of Marquand's writing called *Thirty Years.* Fadiman saw an increasing enlargement in the interests and themes pursued by Marquand.

2. Ambler wrote six spy stories during the late 1930s: *The Dark Frontier, Background to Danger, Epitaph for a Spy, Cause for Alarm, A Coffin for Dimitrios,* and *Journey into Fear. The Dark Frontier* is not well done, and there are also weaknesses in *Epitaph for a Spy.* But the other four are considered by many as classics of their type.

3. Ambler had a number of advantages over Marquand: he avoided limiting himself to a continuing character, escaped the stigma attached to writing magazine serials, worked in a country where spy fiction had precedents, had faithful films of high quality made from his novels, and remained active in the field for some fifty years.

Bibliography

Marquand's Works

The Moto Novels

All works were published by Little, Brown and Company of Boston. This listing is sequentially organized.

No Hero. 1935.
Thank You, Mr. Moto. 1936.
Think Fast, Mr. Moto. 1937.
Mr. Moto Is So Sorry. 1938.
Last Laugh, Mr. Moto. 1942.
Stopover: Tokyo. 1957.

Current Paperbound Reissues

These titles are alphabetized. Little, Brown and Company published all the reissues.

Last Laugh, Mr. Moto. 1986.
Mr. Moto Is So Sorry. 1986.
Right You Are, Mr. Moto. 1986. First published as *Stopover: Tokyo.*
Thank You, Mr. Moto. 1985.
Think Fast, Mr. Moto. 1986.
Your Turn, Mr. Moto. 1985. First published as *No Hero.*

Combination Editions

Mr. Moto: Four Complete Novels. New York: Avenel Books, 1983. The edition contains *Your Turn, Mr. Moto; Think Fast, Mr. Moto; Mr. Moto Is So Sorry;* and *Right You Are, Mr. Moto.*

Mr. Moto's Three Aces: A John P. Marquand Omnibus. Boston: Little, Brown and Company, 1938. The volume includes *Thank You, Mr. Moto; Think Fast, Mr. Moto;* and *Mr. Moto Is So Sorry.*

Thank You, Mr. Moto and Mr. Moto is So Sorry—From the Saturday Evening Post. Indianapolis: The Curtis Publishing Co., 1977.

Serializations

These entries are arranged in the order of publication.

No Hero. Saturday Evening Post, six installments, 30 March through 4 May 1935.

Thank You, Mr. Moto. Saturday Evening Post, six installments, 8 February through 14 March 1936.

Think Fast, Mr. Moto. Saturday Evening Post, six installments, 12 September through 17 October 1936.

Mr. Moto Is So Sorry. Saturday Evening Post, seven installments, 2 July through 13 August 1938.

Mercator Island. Collier's, eight installments, 6 September through 25 October 1941. Published in book form as *Last Laugh, Mr. Moto.*

Rendezvous in Tokyo. Saturday Evening Post, eight installments, 24 November 1956 through 12 January 1957. Published in book form as *Stopover: Tokyo.*

Other Works by Marquand

Thirty Years. Introduction by Clifton Fadiman. Boston: Little, Brown and Company, 1954.

Marquand's major novels are available in many printings.

Selected Studies

Barzun, Jacques, and Wendell H. Taylor. *A Catalogue of Crime.* New York: Harper & Row, Publishers, 1971.

Bell, Millicent. *Marquand: An American Life.* Boston: Little, Brown and Company, 1979.

Birmingham, Stephen. *The Late John Marquand: A Biography.* Philadelphia: J. B. Lippincott Co., 1972.

Breit, Harvey. "An Interview with J. P. Marquand." *New York Times Book Review,* 24 April 1949, p. 35.

Fiske, Constance M. "John P. Marquand." *Saturday Review of Literature*, 10 December 1938, p. 10.

Gross, John J. *John P. Marquand*. New York: Twayne Publishers, Inc., 1963.

Gurko, Leo. "The High Level Formula of J. P. Marquand." *American Scholar* 21 (October 1952), 443–53.

Hamburger, Philip. *J. P. Marquand, Esquire: A Portrait in the Form of a Novel*. Indianapolis: The Bobbs-Merrill Co., Inc., 1952.

Harper, Ralph. *The World of the Thriller*. Cleveland: The Press of Case Western Reserve University, 1969.

Holman, C. Hugh. *John P. Marquand*. Minneapolis: University of Minnesota Press, 1965.

"J. P. Marquand, Esq." *Newsweek*, 7 March 1949, pp. 94–98.

Lardner, John. Review of *B. F.'s Daughter*, *The New Yorker*, 9 November 1946. pp. 117–18.

New York Times. Various editors.

"Spruce Street Boy." *Time*, 7 March 1949, pp. 104–13.

White, William. "Mr. Marquand's 'Mr. Moto.'" *American Speech* 23 (April 1948), 157–58.

"Why Did Mr. Moto Disappear?" *Newsweek*, 21 January 1957, p. 106.

Film Studies

Everson, William K. *The Detective in Film*. Secaucus, N.J.: The Citadel Press, 1972.

Langman, Larry. *A Guide to American Screenwriters: The Sound Era, 1929–1982*. 2 vols. New York: Garland Publishing, Inc., 1984.

Minus, Johnny, and William Storm Hale. *Film Superlist: 20,000 Motion Pictures in the Public Domain*. Hollywood: Seven Arts Press, Inc., 1973.

Mulay, James J., et al., eds. *Spies and Sleuths: Mystery, Spy and Suspense Films on Videocassette*. Evanston, Ill.: CineBooks, Inc., 1988.

The New York Times Encyclopedia of Film. Edited by Gene Brown. 13 vols. New York: Times Books, 1984.

The New York Times Film Reviews, 1913–1968. 6 vols. New York: The New York Times and Arno Press, 1970.

Newsweek. Review of *Stopover Tokyo*, 25 November 1957, p. 122.

Parish, James R., and Michael R. Pitts. *Film Directors: A Guide to Their American Films*. Metuchen, N.J.: The Scarecrow Press, Inc., 1974.

———. *The Great Spy Pictures.* Metuchen, N.J.: The Scarecrow Press, Inc., 1974.

Pitts, Michael R. *Famous Movie Detectives.* Metuchen, N.J.: The Scarecrow Press, Inc., 1979.

Ragan, David. *Who's Who in Hollywood, 1900–1976.* New Rochelle, N.Y.: Arlington House, Publishers, 1976.

Rubenstein, Leonard. *The Great Spy Films.* Secaucus, N.J.: The Citadel Press, 1979.

Sennett, Ted. *Masters of Menace: Greenstreet and Lorre.* New York: E. P. Dutton Co., 1979.

Thomas, Tony, and Aubrey Solomon. *The Films of 20th Century–Fox: A Pictorial History.* Rev. ed. Secaucus, N.J.: The Citadel Press, 1985.

Time. Review of *Mr. Moto's Gamble,* 28 March 1938, p. 38.

Variety Film Reviews. Multivolume. New York: Garland Publishing, Inc., 1983.

Youngkin, Stephen D., et al. *The Films of Peter Lorre.* Introduction by Vincent Price. Secaucus, N.J.: The Citadel Press, 1982.

Filmography

Productions are listed in chronological order, based on release dates, although films were sometimes completed earlier. Lengths are given as a range because figures vary somewhat depending on the source of information and possible variations in prints.

Think Fast, Mr. Moto. Twentieth Century–Fox. 1937.
> Produced by Sol M. Wurtzel.
> Directed by Norman Foster.
> Screenplay by Norman Foster and Howard Ellis Smith.
> Photography by Harry Jackson.
> 66–70 minutes.
> Cast: Peter Lorre, Virginia Field, Sig Rumann, Thomas Beck, J. Carrol Naish, Lotus Long.

Thank You, Mr. Moto. Twentieth Century–Fox. 1937.
> Produced by Sol M. Wurtzel.
> Directed by Norman Foster.
> Screenplay by Norman Foster and Willis Cooper.
> Photography by Virgil Miller.
> 66–68 minutes.
> Cast: Peter Lorre, Pauline Frederick, Philip Ahn, Thomas Beck, Jayne Regan, Sig Rumann, Sidney Blackmer, John Carradine.

Mr. Moto's Gamble. Twentieth Century–Fox. 1938.
> Produced by John Stone.
> Directed by James Tinling.
> Screenplay by Charles Belden and Jerry Cady.
> Photography by Lucien Andriot.
> 60–71 minutes.
> Cast: Peter Lorre, Lynn Bari, Keye Luke, Dick Baldwin, Jayne Regan, Douglas Fowley, Harold Huber, Maxie Rosenbloom, Ward Bond, Lon Chaney, Jr.

Mr. Moto Takes a Chance. Twentieth Century–Fox. 1938.
Produced by Sol M. Wurtzel.
Directed by Norman Foster.
Screenplay by Lou Breslow and John Patrick, from a story by Norman Foster and Willis Cooper.
Photography by Virgil Miller.
57–63 minutes.
Cast: Peter Lorre, Rochelle Hudson, Robert Kent, J. Edward Bromberg, Chick Chandler, George Regas, Fredrik Vogeding.

Mysterious Mr. Moto. Twentieth Century–Fox. 1938.
Produced by Sol M. Wurtzel.
Directed by Norman Foster.
Screenplay by Norman Foster and Philip MacDonald.
Photography by Virgil Miller.
62–65 minutes.
Cast: Peter Lorre, Mary Maguire, Henry Wilcoxon, Erick Rhodes, Harold Huber, Leon Ames, Mitchell Lewis, Forrester Harvey.

Mr. Moto's Last Warning. Twentieth Century–Fox. 1939.
Produced by Sol M. Wurtzel.
Directed by Norman Foster.
Screenplay by Norman Foster and Philip MacDonald.
Photography by Virgil Miller.
71–74 minutes.
Cast: Peter Lorre, Ricardo Cortez, Virginia Field, John Carradine, George Sanders, Joan Carol, John Davidson, Margaret Irving.

Mr. Moto in Danger Island. Twentieth Century–Fox. 1939.
Produced by John Stone.
Directed by Herbert I. Leeds.
Screenplay by Peter Milne.
Photography by Lucien Andriot.
64–70 minutes.
Cast: Peter Lorre, Jean Hersholt, Amanda Duff, Warren Hymer, Richard Lane, Leon Ames, Douglas Dumbrille, Robert Lowery, Paul Harvey.

Mr. Moto Takes a Vacation. Twentieth Century–Fox. 1939.
Produced by the studio.
Directed by Norman Foster.
Screenplay by Norman Foster and Philip MacDonald.
Photography by Charles G. Clarke.
61–65 minutes.

Cast: Peter Lorre, Joseph Schildkraut, Virginia Field, Lionel Atwill, John King, Iva Stewart, John Davidson.

Stopover Tokyo. Twentieth Century–Fox. 1957.
  Produced by Walter Reisch.
  Directed by Richard L. Breen.
  Screenplay by Walter Reisch and Richard L. Breen.
  Photography by Charles G. Clarke.
  100 minutes.
  Cast: Robert Wagner, Joan Collins, Edmond O'Brien, Ken Scott, Reiko Oyama, Larry Keating.

The Return of Mr. Moto. Twentieth Century–Fox. 1965.
  Produced by Robert L. Lippert and Jack Parsons.
  Directed by Ernest Morris.
  Screenplay by Fred Eggers.
  Photography by Basil Emmott.
  71 minutes.
  Cast: Henry Silva, Terence Longdon, Suzanne Lloyd, Marne Maitland, Martin Wyldeck, Stanley Morgan, Harold Kasket.

Index

40, 60; spy fiction, 3–4, 8, 21, 112–115; travels, 7, 12–13, 15–20, 49–50, 57, 65, 70; travels in China, 10, 12, 16, 18–20, 65; travels in Jamaica, 20; travels in Japan, 12, 17, 65; travels in Persia, 20; writing attitudes, style, methods, 11–12, 26, 32, 46, 50–51, 57–59, 61–64, 113.

Maugham, W. Somerset, x.

Mayer, Louis B., 12.

McIntyre, Alfred M., 13, 27, 29, 34, 36, 41, 60; see also Little, Brown and Company.

Melville Goodwin, U.S.A., 14.

Mercator Island, 2, 45–49; see also *Last laugh, Mr. Moto*.

Metro-Goldwyn-Mayer, 12.

Metropolitan Museum of Art, 19.

Miller, Virgil, 92.

Ming Yellow, 11, 26–27, 29.

Mr. Moto, 1–2, 28, 33, 41, 53, 54, 73–74, 76–78, 78–82; career, 76–77, 78–82; clothing, 75; failures, 80–81, see also *Last Laugh, Mr. Moto, Stopover: Tokyo*; nationalism, 77, 78–82; physical appearance, 74–75; professionalism, 77, 78–82; skills, 76–77; speech, 75, 76; ruthlessness, 77, 79–80; see also Mr. Moto films, Mr. Moto novels.

Mr. Moto films, 2–3, 4–5, 89–111, 90–91, 93, 112; see also individual titles.

Mr. Moto in Danger Island, 94, 95, 102.

"Mr. Moto in Egypt," 95.

"Mr. Moto in Puerto Rico," 95.

Mr. Moto Is So Sorry, 2, 40–44, 63–84.

Mr. Moto novels, 1, 2–3, 7, 12–13, 16, 19–20, 26–54, 57–84, 112–115; evaluation, 83–84, 112–115; genre, 3–4, 64–65; heroes, heroines, 66–70; plots, 17, 20, 26–54, 64–67; structure, 65–67; themes, 65–67; see also Mr. Moto, individual titles.

Mr. Moto Takes a Chance, 94, 97–98.

Mr. Moto Takes a Hand, 55; see *No Hero*.

Mr. Moto Takes a Vacation, 94, 102.

Mr. Moto's Gamble, 92, 94, 96–97.

Mr. Moto's Last Warning, 94, 95, 98–101, 106.

Mongolia, 11, 18–19, 28.

"Moto," problem with name, 82–83; use of name during World War II, 83.

Mukden, 17–18.

Murphy, Ray Slater, 19, 36, 69.

Mysterious Mr. Moto, 94.

Naish, J. Carrol, 94.

Newsweek, 50.

New York Times, 17, 102.

No Hero, 2, 26, 27–33, 63–84, 95.

O'Brien, Edmond, 104.

Oland, Warner, 96–97.

Oppenheim, E. Phillips, x, 29.

Outer Mongolia, see Mongolia.

Peking, 10, 16, 18, 19, 20, 34–36, 73, 96; see also China.

Point of No Return, 14.

Priest, Alan, 19, 36.

Puerto Rico, 102.

Pulitzer Prize, 1, 14, 40, 60.

Purpiss, Adams, 18.

Red Mill, The, 52–53, 73.

Regan, Jayne, 94.

Reisch, Walter, 104.

Rendezvous in Tokyo, 2, 51; see also *Stopover: Tokyo*.

Repent in Haste, 14.

Return of Mr. Moto, The, 105.

Riddle of the Sands, The, x.

Right You Are, Mr. Moto, 2; see also *Stopover: Tokyo*.

Rose, Stuart, 49, 50.

Rosenbloom, Maxie, 94, 97.

Rumann, Sig, 94.

Russia, see Union of Soviet Socialist Republics.

Sanders, George, 94, 99–100

Saturday Evening Post, The, 2, 9, 14, 16, 20, 26–45, 49–54, 59–60, 61–63, 73; see also Lorimer, George Horace.

Scaife, Roger, 27.

Schildkraut, Joseph, 94.